THE WAY
OF THE
W A S P

The
WAY
of the
WASP

──────── ✳ ────────

How It Made America,
and How It Can Save It,
So to Speak

Richard Brookhiser

THE FREE PRESS
A Division of Macmillan, Inc.
NEW YORK

Collier Macmillan Canada
TORONTO

Maxwell Macmillan International
NEW YORK   OXFORD   SINGAPORE   SYDNEY

The Free Press
A Division of Macmillan, Inc.
866 Third Avenue, New York, N.Y. 10022

Collier Macmillan Canada, Inc.
1200 Eglinton Avenue East
Suite 200
Don Mills, Ontario M3C 3N1

Printed in the United States of America

printing number

1 2 3 4 5 6 7 8 9 10

Library of Congress Cataloging-in-Publication Data

Brookhiser, Richard.
 The way of the WASP: how it made America, and how it can save it,
so to speak / Richard Brookhiser.
   p.   cm.
 Includes index.
 ISBN 0–02–904721–8
 1. WASPs (Persons)   2. United States—Civilization.
I. Title.
E184.A1B86   1991
305.8'034—dc20   90–38965
                                                          CIP

Page 9: Excerpts from "During Fever" and Waking in the Blue" from *Life Studies* by Robert Lowell. Copyright © 1956, 1959 by Robert Lowell. Reprinted by permission of Farrar, Straus & Giroux, Inc. and Faber & Faber Ltd.

Page 10: Excerpt from "Ringing the Bells" from *To Bedlam and Part Way Back* by Anne Sexton. Copyright © 1960 by Anne Sexton. Reprinted by permission of Houghton Mifflin Co.

For Jeanne

I thought of a rather cruel trick I once played on a wasp. He was sucking jam on my plate, and I cut him in half. He paid no attention, merely went on with his meal, while a tiny stream of jam trickled out of his severed esophagus. Only when he tried to fly away did he grasp the dreadful thing that had happened to him.

GEORGE ORWELL

Contents

Prefatory Note

*S*INCE IN THIS BOOK I will be making a number of (un-
WASPily) blunt identifications, in the interest of (WASPy) fair
play I shall begin by identifying myself.

The Brookhisers were German Catholics. My father's mother's
maiden name was Gleason, which wasn't Irish but a respelling of
Claesgens, another German name (they tried to Anglicize it, evi-
dently, and didn't get it quite right). My mother's maiden name was
Stark (English); her mother's was Quilhot (French Protestant).

I was raised in the Methodist Church, from which I have lapsed. I
grew up in middle-middle-class suburbs and went to Yale. My wife's
maiden name, which she has kept, is Safer (Russian Jew).

For thirteen years, I have worked at *National Review* (Catholic). In
the whole city of New York, I know two Protestants—rather, ex-
Protestants; one of them is Japanese.

Acknowledgments

*M*ANY PEOPLE agreed to sit down and talk with me, including Ken Auletta, Martha Bayles, David Brooks, Jack Cuddihy, Evan Galbraith, George Gilder, Campbell Gibson, Jeffrey Hart, Charles Kesler, Irving Kristol, John Lukacs, Richard Neuhaus, Terry Teachout, and Ernest van den Haag. My thanks to them all. Rich Vigilante has been telling me what to write and think for sixteen years. Why should he stop now?

I owe special debts to Erwin Glikes, for his editorial guidance; to Dan Berk, for his help with research; and to Lou Ann Sabatier, for getting it all in gear.

THE WAY
OF THE
WASP

1

$\star$

Bush-Bashing, WASP-Bashing

*I*F AMERICA NEEDS SAVING, and if only a return to white Anglo-Saxon Protestant behavior and ideals will save it, then aren't we lucky to have George Bush in the White House?

It's a piece of luck we might have counted on, since the presidency is one of the last remaining WASPs-only jobs in America. Van Buren and Roosevelt were not Anglo-Saxon surnames, of course, but since, in New York, the Dutch arrived before the English, they have always been able to pass. Hoover and Eisenhower were once German names, from which, however, all taint of foreignness had been washed by the time their holders ascended to the White House. The lone exception in the long WASP parade was John Kennedy—Roman Catholic and Irish: Roman Catholic, worse than Irish. No one thought of Ronald Reagan, raised in the Christian Church of his mother (née Wilson) as an Irishman, except when he chose to play the role, which was seldom. Given this nearly unbroken string of WASPs, who better to hold such an office, even 370 years after the *Mayflower,* than a descendant of its passengers?

But three years ago things did not look so rosy for George Bush. Though he was Reagan's heir apparent, and though he was seeking the nomination of a party that worships legitimacy, Bush's prospects seemed shaky. They were shaky, because *he* seemed shaky—a shakiness based not so much on anything he said or did, but on who and what he was. Bush's problem was best described by a pair of four-letter words. The word that appeared with depressing regularity in the press was "wimp." The other, the secret synonym, was "WASP." Both made him ripe for bashing.

Partly it was a matter of class. Though few American presidents have actually risen from log cabins, all who can decently do so are obliged to pretend that they have. For Bush the effort was clearly impossible. During a slack period in his pursuit of the White House, I went up to Maine to look at his house. Unlike the out-of-Washington retreats of Richard Nixon, the Bush house on Walker Point in Kennebunkport had not come to him late in life. He had spent every summer of his life there, except for one he had passed in the Pacific in World War II. The Walkers for whom the point was named were the family of his mother, Dorothy. Though George's father, Prescott, had been a Yalie and a member of Skull and Bones, and though he would ultimately become a partner in Brown Brothers, Harriman and a United States senator, in marrying Dorothy Walker he had married up.

The house, its tennis court, its swimming pool, and its assorted outbuildings sit on a knob in the glum Atlantic. The day I hiked past, the only color came from asters and touch-me-nots in the ditches. It is a big place, but not clearly the biggest in the neighborhood. The gentry of Boston and New York have been building up the Maine coast for a century. Sawhorses erected by the Secret Service barred the driveway. Behind them, more imposingly, stood fieldstone gateposts with bronze lamp stands, original work. The seclusion of Walker Point was the seclusion of money, not protection. "Bush," wrote Walt Harrington, a reporter who made the trek up to Walker's Point for the *Washington Post Magazine*, "is of a world apart. . . . Hearing Bush preach the American Gospel—no matter how much I like him—is still like listening to a very tall man praise the virtues of being very tall. I think: *Yeah, that's easy for you to say.*"[1]

But on closer inspection, Bush's class problem had less to do with cash—in the last fifty years, America had put one patrician and one nouveaux, each far richer than Bush, in the White House—than with culture. The damning thing about his background was not that he had lived in Kennebunkport, or Duncannon, South Carolina (the winter house), or Greenwich, Connecticut (the address of record), but what he had learned there. What he had learned was a fusion of reticence and self-control that made him seem inarticulate and insubstantial. Bush's upbringing had made him into a WASP, Eastern elite division. And that made him a wimp.

Newsweek ("Bush Battles the 'Wimp Factor' ") recorded that the report card of the Greenwich Country Day School, which Bush had attended, carried a line, "Claims no more than his fair share of attention." "How'd we do in 'Claims no more'?" was always the first question his father asked of him.[2] In his own campaign autobiography, *Looking Forward,* Bush described a more recent bit of advice from his mother: "'You're talking about yourself too much, George,' she told me after reading a news report covering one of my campaign speeches. I pointed out that as a candidate, I was expected to tell voters something about my qualifications. She thought about that a moment. . . . 'Well, I understand that,' she said, 'but try to restrain yourself.' "[3] Bush's mother had been preaching restraint for years. "If a Bush child burst into the house to say he'd hit a home run that day, Dorothy Bush" (*Newsweek* again) "would sweetly reply, 'How did the *team* do, dear?' "[4] When I told this last anecdote to my wife, who is Jewish, and to a friend, who is Italian, they both reacted as if she had beaten the kid with a shoe. That was also *Newsweek*'s reaction: Note the lethal adverb *sweetly,* which in this context means something closer to *fiendishly.*

The *Los Angeles Times* found a renegade in the Bush clan, a shrink no less, Ray Walker, a cousin of Bush's, to tie it all together. "That is how he relates—by never defining himself against authority. If you have a history of deferring to somebody up the line . . . that's not going to change when you become President."[5] For those skeptical of the conclusions of psychoanalysis—or of envious cousins—there was the testimony of sports. Bush, who had played first base on the Yale baseball team, had a good glove but no bat. "I'd been so wound up in batting techniques—how to meet, pull, hit the ball to the opposite field—that I was swinging defensively." The head groundskeeper in New Haven wrote him a letter: "After watching you play since the season started, I am convinced that the reason you are not getting more hits is because you do not take a real cut at the ball."[6] Bush took his advice and brought his average up to .264.

Bush's stylistic problems affected his substance. Perhaps, indeed, they prevented him from having any. On an evil day, Bush had complained about "the vision thing," a phrase—petulant, incomprehending, and vague—that said it all. "*Vision of the future?*" he had asked rhetorically in *Looking Forward.* "Why would anyone run for President of the United States *without* a comprehensive view of the world? . . . I'll have a lot to say about that after I become a formal candidate and the campaign progresses."[7] But Bush was a candidate, and the campaign had progressed. The world waited.

It's not that the man had no virtues. They were ritually acknowledged: the kids, none (at the time) divorced, of whom it was his proudest boast that they all came home for Christmas; a brave war record; the years of government and political service, however blurry—to which might be added the fact that virtually every journalist who studied him up close came away feeling as much affection as bafflement. But these WASPy strengths came inseparably linked to WASPy weaknesses that canceled them, at least for the task at hand. George Bush was like a great loaded gun that couldn't possibly fire.

February 1988 was the nadir. The caucus-goers of Iowa not only preferred Bob Dole, the senate majority leader, which had been expected. They also preferred Pat Robertson, a sometime faith-healing televangelist without a day's experience in government. "Once a preppy, always a preppy," Reverend Robertson remarked after Bush's third-place finish, as if to say, What did you expect? In New Hampshire, the next state, the *Manchester Union Leader,* eater of candidates, had endorsed Pete du Pont, which wouldn't matter, but it was blasting George Bush as a "spoon-fed rich kid, wet-nursed to success," which might.

Swiftly at first, then slowly and steadily, the low-pressure front of WASPhood lifted. Victory helped. Bush's strength in the GOP had been seriously underestimated. After he won New Hampshire and every Southern primary and caucus, no Republican, at least, would be talking about preppies or spoon-feeding.

For the long haul to November, Bush made an effort subtly to change his background, to jettison his class baggage and travel as a more generic white Anglo-Saxon Protestant. His first feint in that direction had come as early as the preceding summer when, at an all-Republican debate in Houston, he had addressed Pete du Pont as "Pierre." If you're looking for a character from a William Hamilton cartoon, Bush was saying, he's the guy. I'm just an average, English-speaking fellow. A year later Bush's lower-class act picked up steam. The Oak Ridge Boys sang "The Star-Spangled Banner" before one session of the Republican convention in New Orleans. Bush campaigned in rural Illinois at the side of Loretta Lynn. His favorite junk food, it was revealed, the equivalent of Ronald Reagan's jelly beans, was pork rinds. New England, where he had grown up and where he still went to relax, receded. Texas, where he had started in business and politics, came to the fore. His biographical film in New Orleans even noted that he had earned his pilot's wings in Corpus Christi, as if his being there had been an instance of philo-Southernism, rather than a military assignment.

His most important maneuver, however, was to shift the burden of background onto his opponent, to raise questions about someone else's world view and fitness to rule. The Democratic party obliged by nominating Michael Dukakis, a man from a strange and distant land. Not Greece, of course, but Brookline, Massachusetts.

I had gone to look at Dukakis's house the same day I inspected Bush's (they are only ninety minutes apart by car). Brookline was the home of the first country club, and Henry Pulham, the narrator of a J. P. Marquand novel, grew up on a 60-acre estate there. But over the years suburbs and urbs had filled it in. Dukakis's street was neat, slumbrous, and residential. There were two small apartment buildings on one end of his block. The rest was houses, sixty years old or more, topped with odd little widow's walks, sharing their tiny lots with tall trees. A few of the driveways were unsurfaced, which I took to be a sign of chic. Plastic trash bags lined the curbs, bulging with pine needles and chestnuts.

It didn't look dangerous. But the menace, the Bush campaign would argue, lay in the beliefs of the inhabitants. The bumper stickers on the parked cars—"SAVE THE WHALES, WE'RE HORSE PEOPLE"—gave a clue to Brookline's allegedly disabling abnormality. Dukakis's record as governor (or selected bits of it, endlessly harped upon) supplied the rest.

Brookline—very sophisticated, very sure of itself, and very uninterested in hoi polloi—was the context, the missing link between the furlough of Willie Horton, the veto of the Pledge of Allegiance, and all the other Republican low-road one-shots of the fall campaign. The man who lives there, and who condones these things, so the Bush argument ran, doesn't know about normal America, doesn't know about real life. He worships strange gods.

Many Dukakis supporters wished he would answer the attack on his world view and his neighborhood with a little Greek fire. They had the wrong man. There was little that was ethnic about Dukakis's style or his base of support. About 17 percent of Dukakis's prenomination war chest had come from Greek-Americans—a solid sum, but nowhere near a lion's share. He had raised most of his money from Harvard alumni who had lived in his state; from New York money men he had dealt with as governor; and from entrepreneurs plugged into the Massachusetts hi-tech industry. The election, he had promised, would be about competence, and that is the way he ran his campaign. "The cold Brookline winters," complained the columnist Richard Cohen, "have stolen his Medi-

terranean sun." He "conduct[s] himself as if he were running for
First Dentist."[8] Dukakis's even demeanor, it had seemed early on in
the race, might armor him against ideological assault. "How can his
heart be bleeding," asked one pundit, "if no one's sure it's even
beating?"[9] But when the Republicans went ahead and assaulted
him anyway, Dukakis fell calmly into the trap.

So Bush kept his sights firmly on Brookline, not on ethnicity, on
Dukakis's address, not his roots. Consider the Bush campaign's
treatment of the subject that had been the warhead issue against
Kennedy and Al Smith: religion. On two occasions Michael and
Kitty Dukakis's faiths—Greek Orthodoxy and Judaism, respectively—were attacked by free-lance conservative advocates. The
grounds of the assaults, however, were that neither of the Du-
kakises was faithful enough. Jim Jatras, a Republican Senate aide
and a Greek Orthodox believer, complained that Michael Dukakis
had left his religion by raising his children outside it. Don Feder, a
conservative columnist for the *Boston Herald*, leveled the same
charge at Kitty. The Dukakis family line—that the children were
being raised in both "cultures"—did not satisfy the two believers. It
was a long way from 1960, when John Kennedy was forced to
journey to Houston to abjure Guelphism. The charges, however,
provoked such a storm in favor of a third American faith, more
potent than Orthodoxy or Judaism—lukewarmness—that the
critics backed off. For the rest, the Bushmen left their opponent's
ethnicity alone.[10]

When the returns were in, and the ex-wimp turned out to be the
winner, a new thought occurred to handicappers of ethnicity:
Bush's WASPishness had been a blessing, not a hindrance. Bush's
strongest campaign suit, it seemed, wasn't Willie Horton, but Ralph
Lauren. "For more than a decade," wrote Alessandra Stanley in a
postelection issue of *The New Republic*, "Lauren has been hooking
middle class and lower middle class Americans on WASP aesthetics
and pseudo-English gentility; the country has gone from Ralph
Lauren clothes, to Ralph Lauren house furnishings, to Ralph Lau-
renesque architecture, design, and art. Get ready for the Ralph
Lauren presidency."[11] Clothes make the man. The Polo line imposed on America a false consciousness—a WASP consciousness.

It is easy to be wise after the fact. It is a pity that Stanley, who
covered the campaign for *Time*, did not vouchsafe her insights to
her colleagues at *Newsweek et al.* back in the days of the wimp factor.
At best, America's attitude to George Bush's WASPery was ambiva-

lent. He had managed his WASP problem by evasion as much as by persuasion.

If Bush's election did not represent a clear-cut victory for WASPs and their ways, then perhaps that procession of white Anglo-Saxon Protestant presidents is also misleading, a fossil of old habits, not an accurate indicator of the way we live now. It's not as if George Bush was the first WASP to be bashed. Culturally, Ralph Lauren is a ripple. For sixty years the country's intellectual leaders and followers have been laboring to unhook middle- and lower-middle- (and upper-) class America from WASP anything.

Take H. L. Mencken. Mencken is perhaps the lone example in American cultural history of an obstreperous German. He made up for a lot. "What are the characters that I discern most clearly in the so-called Anglo-Saxon type of man? . . . Two stick out above all others. One is his curious and apparently incurable incompetence—his congenital inability to do any difficult thing easily and well, whether it be isolating a bacillus or writing a sonata. The other is his astounding susceptibility to fears and alarms—in short, his hereditary cowardice. . . . Civilization is at its lowest mark in the United States precisely in those areas where the Anglo-Saxon still presumes to rule. . . . There we look for such pathological phenomena as Fundamentalism, Prohibition and Ku Kluxery, and there they flourish." But since Mencken also called non–Anglo Saxon Americans "botched and unfit"—"Irishmen starving to death in Ireland, Germans unable to weather the *Sturm und Drang* of the post-Napoleonic reorganization, Italians weed-grown on exhausted soil, Scandinavians run to all bone and no brain, Jews too incompetent to swindle even the barbarous peasants of Russia, Poland, and Roumania"[12]—he may not be the steadiest compass on the subject.

A better starting place is D. H. Lawrence's assault on Benjamin Franklin. It preceded Mencken's fireworks, and it was subtler and more serious. Of all the Founding Fathers, Franklin might have seemed the most congenial to modern times—the least stiff and plastered, tinkering with kites and stoves, and writing flirtatious letters to Frenchwomen in his old age. Lawrence knew better. Mencken attacked WASPs for their vices; Lawrence flayed Franklin for his virtues. "I can remember, when I was a little boy, my father to buy a scrubby yearly almanac. . . . Crammed in corners it had little anecdotes and humorisms, with a moral tag. And I used to

have my little priggish laugh at the woman who counted her
chickens before they were hatched and so forth, and I was convinced that honesty was the best policy, also a little prig-
gishly. . . . And probably I haven't got over those Poor Richard tags
yet. I rankle still with them. They are thorns in young flesh."
Why? "I am a moral animal. But I am not a moral machine. I don't
work with a little set of handles or levers. The Temperance-
silence-order-resolution-frugality-industry-sincerity-justice-mod-
eration-cleanliness-tranquillity-chastity-humilty keyboard"—Lawrence refers to a list of virtues Franklin drew up in his twenties—"is
not going to get me going. . . . As for his Godhead, his Providence,
He is head of nothing except a vast heavenly store."[13] Lawrence's
search for better gods would take him to the Aztecs.

Mencken was what might nowadays be called an ethnic, and
Lawrence was a foreigner. The chorus of complaint was joined
early on, and sustained all along, by unhappy WASPs themselves.
John P. Marquand made a career as the bard of WASP civilization
and its discontents, making the case comically, and most successfully, in *The Late George Apley* (1936), the story of a proper
Bostonian, admirable in certain respects, but so bound in the
strictures of his upbringing that he never gets anything he truly
wants. He can't join a club unless his father approves; he can't have
a fishing camp in Maine without his wife taking it over, and anyway
he shouldn't have married her but the Irish girl he fell in love with
in college. As the years and novels passed, Marquand dropped the
humor, until by *Point of No Return* (1950), things are very grim
indeed. Charles Gray (get it?)—"He's a nice boy," a friend of his, an
anthropologist, remarks, "he has that repressed quality"[14]—attains
exactly what he has wanted all his professional life, the vice-presi-
dency of a bank, and it is ashes in his mouth.

The testimony of renegade WASPs would always be useful,
though it was aesthetically suspect, given its source. James Gould
Cozzens spent years passing on ammunition about adultery, embezzlement, and other WASP derelictions, accumulating an enormous reputation thereby until 1958, when Dwight Macdonald, in
one review in *Commentary,* having decided that Cozzens was as
leaden and unattractive as his subjects, capsized him: "inhib-
ited . . . frightened by feeling . . . defen[ded] against emotion
. . . Dickens, Tolstoy, and other novelists have written law-court
scenes showing that truth is too small a fish to be caught in the law's

coarse meshes. But to Cozzens, a trial is reality while emotional, disorderly life is the illusion."[15]

Lowbrow is always a lagging indicator, but in 1956 *Peyton Place* revealed goings-on north of Boston that ought not to have gone on. Movies, the great furnace of WASPification—in which Daniel Kaminsky came out Danny Kaye, and Issur Danielovitch Kirk Douglas—also began to catch on. *David and Lisa* showed what having an ice queen WASP mother did to you—it made you mad, like poor David. Robert Lowell reported similar results. "Terrible that old life of decency/without unseemly intimacy/or quarrels, when the unemancipated woman/still had her Freudian papá and maids!" When things got bad enough, you ended up in a madhouse whose attendants were students from Boston College. "There are no Mayflower/screwballs in the Catholic Church."[16]

On the threshold of the sixties, Norman Mailer found that WASP mental illness caused illness: " . . . the Protestant is the historical embodiment of the great will which deadened the flesh (in all cruelty and no taste, one must admit that cancer has been their last contribution to civilization)." Our only hope was that "the Negro emerge . . . as a dominating force in American life"—not in the form in which Negroes actually emerged, minister politicians, but as cognoscenti of "perversion, promiscuity, pimpery, drug addiction, rape, razor-slash, bottle-break, what-have-you," from which they had elaborated "a morality of the bottom."[17]

In 1964 WASPs—rich, powerful ones anyway—came in for serious scholarly treatment. E. Digby Baltzell's *The Protestant Establishment*, laden with historical and sociological tidbits, makes interesting reading today, despite the oddity of its thesis. "All over the world, the people, if not always their leaders, look to America for leadership. But America's continuing authority in the world depends on our ability to solve the problem of authority here at home." And who had caused that? "A crisis in moral authority has developed in modern America largely because of the White-Anglo-Saxon-Protestant establishment's unwillingness, or inability, to continuously absorb . . . talented and distinguished members of minority groups into its privileged ranks."[18] A sobering thought. All over the world, Serbs and Croats, Hutu and Tutsi, Brahmins and Untouchables, Israelis and Arabs, Afrikaners and Zulus, the IRA and the Orange Order would harden their hearts against us because Jews had to join the Harmonie Club.

The sixties—not the chronological sixties but the cultural sixties, roughly from the murder of John Kennedy to the resignation of Richard Nixon—was a heyday of WASP entomology. Louis Auchincloss's Rector found that the alumni of Justin were bigoted, materialistic oafs. Eldridge Cleaver announced that "the white youth of today" were tired "of dragassing across the dance floor like zombies to the dead beat of mind-smothered Mickey Mouse music."[19] Norman Podhoretz described the "brutal bargain" of cultural upward mobility—of "making it"—and his own near escape from its most brutal clause: "becoming a facsimile WASP."[20] Garry Wills paid a visit to Richard Nixon's Quaker hometown, Whittier, California, and did not much like what he saw. "Nixon is President of the forgotten men, of those affluent displaced persons who howled at Wallace rallies, heart-broken, moneyed, without style. . . . The 'forgotten America' is helpless, in its need, against excess and tastelessness."[21] Michael Novak keened for Catholic Slavs, round pegs in square WASP holes: "What has happened to my people since they came to this land nearly a century ago? . . . Will we ever find that secret relief, that door, that hidden entrance? Did our grandparents choose for us, and our posterity, what they should have chosen?" Sex was better in the Catholic old countries, displaying "lyricism, freedom, naturalness, trembling, and the cultivation—not of techniques—but of communion."[22] So was Jewish sex here. It took twenty-two pages, but Harold Brodkey's Wiley finally got Orra Perkins to come for the first time. Ben Stein, interviewing TV writers and producers in the seventies, found deep reserves of antipathy for the small-town WASP (the Waltons aside). "I've heard a lot of stories about Jews being beat up in small towns," one writer explained. "This is not paranoia. It really happened. There are a lot of dumb, violent people in small towns." When asked if she considered small towns frightening, a producer "at first said 'No,' and then added, 'Jesus, they did vote for Nixon.'"[23]

WASPs kept on firing away at themselves. Anne Sexton joined Lowell in spilling (New England) beans: "we mind by instinct,/like bees caught in the wrong hive," she wrote of women in a madhouse, though her readers took it, correctly, to apply to a whole class. Jim Morrison, a Methodist Air Force brat from Florida, made a career singing about love, madness, and parricide. The Doors were one of the groups that marked the shift of rock (which had always been a part-WASP enterprise) from energy to angst. Jerry Lee Lewis had set pianos on fire because it was fun. The Doors were Serious. Coincidentally, the music got worse. "Great Balls of Fire" is a much better song than "Come On, Baby, Light My Fire."[24]

As the sixties wore out their welcome, so to a degree did the great WASP hunt. The thought sprang up, simultaneously and independently, in many a mind: Rattling the pillars was fun, but suppose everything actually did come down? Peter Schrag, in a book entitled *The Decline of the WASP,* approached his subject as a not-entirely-happy Samson: Amid the barks at Southern football games and Sunday dinners at Holiday Inns and Coach Houses ("these are not Frenchmen or Italians making love to their food, enveloping it, surrounding and overwhelming it") there sounded a rueful note: "the WASP ethic and culture were the essential elements of our Americanism. We are losing them, and are therefore losing ourselves."[25] Even Norman Mailer came to look on the inventors of cancer with "a sad sorrowful respect," though he still found them disproportionately afflicted with "dowager's hump," "flaccid paunch," and mouths "forever locked in readiness to bite the tough meat of resistance."[26]

Throughout the eighties, the direct fire lightened to a patter. Richard C. Robertiello, MD, complained (in *The Wasp Mystique*) that he had a bad time at WASP dinner parties: "very foreign affair[s] to the newcomer on the scene; as the non-WASP author of this book can attest. First he will have a difficult time working his way into the conversation because there are rarely any breaks at which he might be able to enter with his comments. When he does finally speak he will feel like he is either holding court, because everyone's attention will be turned toward him on account of his awkward manner of breaking into the conversation, or he quite simply will be ignored."[27] Robert Christopher, in a genial update of *The Protestant Establishment,* said it was all a mistake. Everybody was in the establishment now, and it hadn't been all that WASPy to begin with anyway: "America was invented and built not just by Anglo-Saxon Protestants but by people of diverse ethnic origins and religious beliefs."[28] Jackie Mason explained why WASPS, alone among ethnic groups, have no cockroaches: because there's no food in the house. It takes an individual WASP, showing unseemly presumption, such as George Bush, to provoke a general bombardment.

One particular WASP subgroup, however, enjoys no peace: the evangelical fundamentalist born-agains. On them it has been open season since the Scopes Trial—when they have been noticed at all.

Mencken is more pertinent here, for on this subject his prejudices never wavered. He dismissed all religions with the ease of the home-made philosophe; he dismissed Christianity most emphatically, as the religion which daily annoyed him; he dismissed Protestantism more contemptuously than Catholicism, since it was plainer and more literal, and hence dumber and more dangerous; when his prose could wrap itself around low church, Bible-beating true believers, it was a marriage made in heaven. For years, he catalogued their foibles: ignorance, tyranny, suspicion, fear, sexual repression. Most gleefully the last. Here he is, peeping at a prayer meeting:

> From the squirming and jabbering mass a young woman
> gradually detached herself—a woman not uncomely, with a
> pathetic homemade cap on her head. . . . Presently her whole
> body began to be convulsed—great throes that began at the
> shoulders and ended at the hips. Her praying flattened out
> into a mere delirious caterwauling. I describe the thing discreetly, and as a strict behaviorist. The lady's subjective sensations I leave to infidel pathologists, privy to the works of
> Ellis, Freud, and Moll. Whatever they were, they were obviously not painful, for they were accompanied by vast heavings and gurglings of a joyful and even ecstatic nature.[29]

The theme of battered born-again libido is a favorite of the enlightened, appearing in their writings whenever fundamentalists do, as in the divinity school where one of John Updike's narrators teaches: "an unattractive lot they tend to be, with a curious physical propensity for wall eyes and jugears and among the females, enormous breasts, which they carry through our halls like a penitential weight."[30]

Famous evangelicals fare no better. When Jimmy Carter, a self-proclaimed born-again, first ran for president, literate America gaped at the prodigy. Carter did his best to give no offense, but subsequent evangelicals in the political realm had an even harder time of it. Jerry Falwell, founder of the Moral Majority, was routinely linked, in street demonstration signs and magazine sidebars, with Jim Jones and the Ayatollah Khomeini. Falwell's beliefs about the scenario for the Second Coming struck an editor of *The New Republic* as "mad," "bonkers," "rattle-brained tripe." When Pat Robertson ran for president, the same writer speculated that he suffered from psychotic delusions.[31] Almost no cultured person, apart from pundits of the right, had a good word to say for either of them. Garry Wills, recovered from his visit to Whittier, was an exception: He came within an inch of proposing Pat Robertson to the *Christian Century* as the most important religious figure of 1988, though in the end he plumped for Jesse Jackson.

Prejudice against this sort of WASP infects the analysis of even the most fair-minded. In the midst of a discussion of civility and fanaticism, the sociologist John Murray Cuddihy reaches in passing for instances, and comes up with three pairs of theologians, one Protestant, one Roman Catholic, one Jewish. "Scratch a Niebuhr and you'll find a Billy Graham; scratch a Murray and find a Feeney; scratch a Hertzberg and find a Kahane."[32] Reinhold Niebuhr, John Courtney Murray, and Arthur Hertzberg naturally represent civility. Graham, Leonard Feeney, and Meier Kahane are the clods. But look again at the clods. Leonard Feeney was a Boston Jesuit, excommunicated for extreme traditionalism, who retired to the Massachusetts countryside with a small band of disciples. Kahane, founder of the Jewish Defense League, was a political figure so marginal in this country that he took himself to Israel, where he was ultimately banned from politics. Their Protestant counterpart in oddball fanaticism, as Cuddihy sees it, has been a mainstay for thirty years of Most-Admired lists and White House guest lists. It looks as if Cuddihy were being casually unfair, as out of touch with a huge slice of American life as only a professor at Hunter can be. Yet he is right. To another slice of American life—the slice that would be apt to read his book—Graham is seen in just that way.

Evangelical religion, finally, is hopelessly lower—make that lowest—class. "WHAT CLASS ARE YOU?" asks the inside cover of Paul Fussell's *Class*. "*Your Vocabulary Shouts It*." There follows a list of characteristic phrases, correctly identified: "UPPER 'Grandfather died' MIDDLE 'Grandma passed away' PROLE 'Uncle was taken to Jesus.'"[33] You may get to Heaven, but you'll have to go in by the servants' entrance.

Here then is the indictment, a sample of the bill of particulars against the WASP. This, not any daydream fostered by Ralph Lauren, is how white Anglo-Saxon Protestants and their history and habits are actually written and thought about these days. They didn't have as much impact on this country as we've always been led to believe, but what they had was unfortunate. They give everyone else a hard time, an offense mitigated, if it is mitigated, only by the hard time they give themselves. They are breeders of disease and founts of pathology. They're bad dancers and lousy lays, and they make Dr. Robertiello feel uncomfortable at meals. The food would have been inedible anyway. Their upper classes can still win presidential elections (though only with the help of Jewish clothes designers), but they can't hit baseballs; their lower classes profess religions that are little better than voodoo, and a lot less fun. For three and a half centuries, they have suffered in silence and lashed out in self-righteous rages. But they have done worse—they have offered themselves, with surprising success, considering their inherent unwholesomeness, as models. They do not simply float, like some sharp-edged impervious ice floe, in the national current; they have lowered the water temperature for everybody else. They have done their best to make America unlivable, and they have made it a byword among nations.

These aren't the effusions of cranks, of the Nation of Islam on whites or the Aryan Nation on blacks. This is a broad consensus of literary gents, some eminent, many popular; of experts and would-be experts in the field; of purveyors of mass culture, with the occasional crazy man—Norman Mailer, the early Cleaver—thrown in, but not at all out of place. It has been disseminated by blockbusters and little magazines, movies and television. It is broad-brush and mainstream.

It also happens to be wrong. Some counts of the indictment are contradictory on their face (how can a group be simultaneously tangential and omnipotent?). Others rest on simple misjudgments. Take the universal belief in WASP rigidity. True enough, perhaps, in some situations—on the dance floor or in the batter's box. But not in others. In debate, it was Dukakis who was frigid, knotted with inhibitions, and ill at ease; Bush was the responsive one, even if his responses were at times irrelevant or off the wall. Hence, in large measure, the envy and resentment Bush excites. (Who envies a stiff?) Many WASP deficiencies, finally, as with the elements of any stereotype, turn out on closer inspection to be truly observed and truly deficient. But on closest inspection, they also turn out to be shadows, reflections of strengths. Their vices are the vices of their virtues. And their virtues make an impressive collection.

If this were a matter of relevance only to WASPs, it would hardly be worth recording (certainly not for WASPs—boasting is the vice of no virtue). But it is relevant to Americans, not just Bushes and Baltzells, but Brookhisers and Gleasons as well. The genial Mr. Christopher is wrong, the saturnine Mr. Schrag is right. The WASP character is the American character. It is the mold, the template, the archetype, the set of axes along which the crystal has grown. Without the WASP, it would be another country altogether. Without the continuing influence of his values, it is sure to lose its way.

This is, I realize, an eccentric interpretation of American exceptionalism. There are many competing ones to choose from. An old favorite holds that America's character was determined by its frontiers. Wide open space made American society wide open. Fanaticism in Europe, wrote St. John de Crèvecoeur, "is confined; here it evaporates in the great distance it has to travel; there it is a grain of powder inclosed, here it burns away in the open air, and consumes without effect."[34] A smaller country would have been less free. Intellectual cousins of the frontiersmen are the immigrationists, who see America as the sum of its heterogeneous parts, a composite of the peoples who filled the wilderness or were sucked into the settled parts of the country in the wake of the departing pioneers.

There are also partisans of ideological explanations of the American thing: that it was the first, and fairest, fruit of the Enlightenment; that it was the first, or second, modern democracy (depending on how democratic the pre-Reform Mother of Parliaments is held to have been); that it is the twin sibling of capitalism, whose Declaration of Independence was published the same year as *The Wealth of Nations* (said with as many groans as hosannas).

These alternative explanations, material or intellectual, miss the mark. The frontier is too crude, the others are too abstract. A country is not the acres of dirt of which it physically consists, but the people upon them; and the best guide to understanding them is their character, not the names they give their systems. Their character shapes their systems. Russia had a huge frontier; so did Argentina and South Africa, which also attracted millions of immigrants. America is unlike any of them; it is not all that much like Canada, also big, barren, and settled by outsiders. Capitalism has flourished in all sorts of places, from Hamburg to Hong Kong, without turning them into little Americas. Democracy takes even more peculiar forms. India is a democracy. So is Haiti, off and on. East Germany—the German Democratic Republic—called itself one, even while the Wall was still up. The latter society was undoubtedly a product of the Enlightenment—a different line, certainly, but an equally legitimate one.

The American is not a *homo economicus* or *democraticus*. He is not what he is because he sat in a salon or tramped through the wilderness. His nature is more particular than a theory or a circumstance. It has a local habitation and a name. And that is, that he was once a WASP. To miss this is to get everything else wrong; it is like listening to music with an ear infection. Political rhetoric about a return to values and academic chatter about habits of the heart become idle. One slights what we have and misjudges what we can become.

From the early seventeenth to the late eighteenth century, America was created by what are known, for lack of a better term, as white Anglo-Saxon Protestants. They wrote the rules; everyone else played by them. If America had been settled and founded by Frenchmen or Spaniards, as it might well have been, or by the Austrian Empire or the Ashanti Empire, to be purely hypothetical, it would be a different place now. And a worse one. This book will make that case.

Any project to improve or repair the country the WASPs made should be attentive to its particular patterns of thought and forms of behavior. If the only living and healthy values to which the whole country has access are WASP values, then anything restorative or profitable we try to accomplish has to draw on them. This book will also make that case.

Are these cases, finally, worth making? Since George Bush is in the White House and Reverend Graham is well known outside Hunter, does it matter what their cultured despisers—acknowledging that culture includes schlock novels as well as sociological treatises—think?

If low opinions of WASPs and their works are confined to a minority, it is still an articulate minority. If its prejudices go unchallenged, then America is in the position of doing one thing and saying another. It cannot speak its mind; it cannot think its mind.

But things are worse than that. I propose to show that the low opinions of WASPs I have catalogued—from D. H. Lawrence to the last election coverage—are only symptoms, not causes, of a deeper mental shift. For decades—for a century, in some cases—Americans have been turning away from WASP ways of thinking and behaving, with disastrous results. At first the turn was an elite trickle, but in the last twenty years it has become a stampede. Products of a social and cultural machine that works as well as anything humanly can, Americans have ineptly tried to fix it. Hip-deep in blessings that the rest of the world covets, they have thrown them away with both hands. The worst tinkerers and spendthrifts have been actual WASPs themselves. As a result of their feckless-ness, the WASP character, which is the American character, has shattered. And since the world does not hold many better ones—or if it does, it has kept them well hidden—a cry for restoration is in order. Or at least a lament.

America was made by the way of the WASP, though many Ameri-cans, WASPs included, have recently abandoned it. This book will urge them to return to it, in a manner more decisive than a simple vote of the Electoral College.

2

★

Who Are These People?

*E*ARLY ON in one of the novels of Louis Auchincloss, a WASP nips into Trinity Church, at the head of Wall Street, to consider his deteriorating financial position—he is, indeed, about to be caught red-handed in embezzlement—but finds himself thinking instead of what both the church and his family stand for: "the survival of a small, tough piece" of old New York "on an island overwhelmed with the old poor of the old world and the new rich of the new. Of course," he thinks on, "Trinity was not itself very old," having been "designed in the eighteen-forties by the same Upjohn who had built my grandfather's Newport villa. . . . "[1]

Probably there are still people like that. Certainly there are still books about people like that, written and read by those who assume that WASPs are solely the rich and more-than-famous (for there are some celebrities so arcane that one has to achieve a certain eminence even to be aware of their existence). So a sizable literature of the WASP *vieux riche* has sprung up, half gossip, half wish fulfillment—authors' gossip, readers' wish fulfillment. It can be interesting. It can even be funny, as its most sophisticated purveyors realize. Nelson W. Aldrich, Jr., spends half his book *Old Money* relishing the irony of its title, since his money is no older than his great-grandfather, the nineteenth-century son of a mill hand. Compared to the latest Count von Thurn und Taxis, boogeying in *W*, whose family were postmasters of the Holy Roman Empire, anything in America, especially money, is brand new.

But this is too tight a focus for seeing anything as broad as a national character type. Elites are important, especially when, unlike present-day counts, they actually lead. But they are not the

19

whole story. In a society in which elites circulate with any speed, there has to be a mental kinship between those at the top and those who may soon be. The on-deck circle must resemble the batter's box. In a society that is to any extent democratic, there has to be a general community of feeling. Otherwise leaders could not lead. A Spartan Louis Auchincloss could ignore the helots without fear of missing anything important. But America is not Sparta.

The first definition to make, then, is that the word WASP includes all of WASPdom: the whole loaf, not just the upper crust. We want to understand people in Akron and Arkansas, not just Andover; United Methodists and members of the Church of the Nazarene, not just Episcopalians; people who clip supermarket coupons as well as the ones who clip the coupons of trust funds.

Another preliminary point, more important than it seems, concerns orthography. How should we spell WASP, with all caps or as an acronym that has congealed into a word? Digby Baltzell, who coined the term, used capitals, but he apparently sets no great store by the word. He invented it, he told me, "because it fit on a chart."[2] "Wasp," with only the "W" upper-cased, has the sanction of Norman Mailer to recommend it. It is also less ugly. Pages covered with clumps of capital letters look like press releases of the Department of Defense (DoD). Finally, the image of the insect—swarming, unpredictable, dangerous—was essential to the term's popularity. An acronym that spelled out Ants or Crickets would not have been nearly as useful as a weapon of cultural warfare.

WASP, however unsightly, has the great advantage of highlighting the constituent parts. Each—W, AS, and P—is important (the order of importance is ascending). I shall use all four letters, all capitalized, throughout.

Who are the WASPs in America today? Anyone asking such a question will find a mass of data in the Census. He will also find numerous pitfalls for the unwary.

Whites are easy enough to calculate. The race question of the last (1980) Census asked, "Is this person White, Black or Negro, Japanese, Chinese, Filipino . . . " and so on, through eight more "races," down to Aleut.

With Anglo-Saxons the fun begins. Over the years the Census has put a variety of questions related to ethnicity: country of origin, country of parents' origin, language, mother tongue. In many cases the relationship is quite faint: What did coming from the Austro-Hungarian Empire say about an immigrant's *ethnos*? In 1980 the

Census baldly asked, With what ancestry group did one identify? If a person gave a double-barreled answer (Irish-Italian) he was counted as two ethnics; the most common combinations of three yielded three identities.

Toting up these results, the Census reported 49.6 million Americans identifying themselves, in whole or part, as of English descent (Scottish, 10 million, and Welsh, 1.6 million, were separate categories). Germans came in a close second, with 49.2 million. Irish were third, at just over 40 million. "Black or Negro" (26.8 million) was fourth, while 20 million Americans had no thoughts on the matter. The 1990 Census, whose ancestry numbers will not be crunched for two more years, is expected to show large rises in Americans of Oriental and Latin American descent. But this will not effect rankings at the top.

Asking for self-identification is asking for trouble, and the Census data are indeed filled with weird results. The county with the highest proportion of Turks, for example, turned out to be in South Carolina, "Turks" being the local name for an ingrown community of black, white, and Indian ancestry. They worship in their own Baptist church, and they are about as Turkish as Michael Dukakis. Yet the Census lumps them with new arrivals from Ankara.

Other categories are undercounted—including English. English ancestry, says Bruce Chapman, a former director of the Census, is "like a base coat of paint: anything that goes over it is more interesting."[3] The main repository of hidden English-Americans is the seventh largest category identified by the Census, ahead of Scottish and just behind Italian—the almost 12 million Americans who called themselves "Americans." Stanley Lieberson, a sociologist at Berkeley, guesses that "a sizable segment" of these are "some sort of British origin—that is, they are disproportionately Southern Protestants with at least four generations of residence in the United States."[4]

On Protestants, the Census is mum. For the last half-century, it has been considered a breach of the wall of separation to ask anything about religion. The bureau asked some religious questions in a between-censuses survey in 1957 but, in response to protest, published none of its conclusions and destroyed the data.

Sociologists can give more information about WASPs—a little more. WASPs are not a popular subject. As Joseph Adelson, at the University of Michigan, notes, "you really don't get WASPs going into the social sciences. Even when they do, they don't deal with themselves."[5] When WASPs are studied, they may yield unwanted results. Edwin Harwood did his doctoral dissertation at the University of Chicago in 1966 on poor Southern whites living in the Uptown section of Chicago. "There was a lot of interest in them just then," Harwood recalls, "because people could say, 'Ah, there are *white* poor.'" But it turned out that the urban hillbillies were "making quite an adequate adjustment. They greatly resented the Yankee press trying to portray them as helpless people requiring the full panoply of government assistance."[6]

But if our main interest in WASPs is as archetypes, then the most important WASPs are not the ones we have but the ones we had in 1776 and 1620. We must look at the founding generations, at the the people who wrote the rules, and see what the acronym meant two and three hundred years ago.

WHITE

In early America, white meant not red and not black. It meant, therefore, everyone who was in a position to shape the colonies' and the new country's institutions.

Indians permeate American mythology, but they are a sideshow of American history. They have lately taken to calling themselves Native Americans, and they are certainly native. But "Americans" is an anachronism. America was an invention of European mapmakers. America fought Indians, displaced them, and finally impounded them. It did not include them.

Blacks raise a more interesting question, as far as WASPs are concerned, for they lived from the beginning in a WASP world, though they were compelled to occupy an inferior role in it. Black culture and WASP culture crossed at a multitude of points, from food to worship. But despite their proximity, black slaves were in no position to shape the institutions of WASP society directly.

ANGLO-SAXON

The slipperiest letters in WASP are the A and the S.

The Angles and the Saxons were two of the barbarian tribes that overran Roman Britain. In the mid-nineteenth century those terms of history acquired a political resonance due to the cultural and nationalistic aspirations of Germany, England, and the United States. English and American scholars who went to get their doctorates at German universities came home eager to imagine some kind of cultural connection. "English and American historians," says the historian John Lukacs wryly, "discovered that Anglo-Saxon liberties came from the German forests."[7] Edward Bulwer Lytton, the man who ruined the ending of *Great Expectations,* wrote a weepy historical novel, *Harold: Last of the Saxon Kings,* in which Anglo-Saxon virtue falls at the Battle of Hastings to Norman vice. (I found an old copy in my grandmother's house.) When England decided, later in the century, that Germany might be a rival, not a blood brother, and that the Empire's security depended on American friendship, Anglo-Saxonism became the rationale for Anglo-American partnership, epitomized by a trans-Atlantic trade in American brides, one of whom produced Winston Churchill.

The myth-making was abetted and justified by a bogus ethnic anthropology. The last half of the nineteenth century and the first quarter of this one were the heyday of measuring skull sizes and the slope of foreheads. Hence the currency of words like braciocephalic, which pop up in the tales of Arthur Conan Doyle.

If it were not too late in the day, it would be better to abandon the phrase, and substitute Anglo-American, or English. But since it is too late, we must proceed, mindful of the absurdities.

"By 1740," wrote J. C. Furnas, America's "ethnic hand was dealt for the next few generations."[8] What was it?

The first Americans were not a homogeneous lot. There had been non-English settlements in what became the Thirteen Colonies, and not all the immigrants to England's colonies came from England. In 1644 the Dutch governor of New Netherland told a visitor that his subjects spoke eighteen languages. When the Dutch captured New Sweden on the Delaware River eleven years later, they picked up two more, Swedish and Finnish. The largest non–English-speaking group consisted of German peasants who settled most heavily in Pennsylvania, where they constituted an ethnic plurality. There were variations even among those who came as subjects of the English crown. So many Scottish Highlanders came to upcountry North Carolina that the postmasters of Fayetteville were obliged to know Gaelic until well into the nineteenth century.

Still, the Thirteen Colonies were heavily English. Guessing a country's ethnic composition two hundred years ago is no easier than counting it today. The best method historians have come up with is extrapolating from the frequency of characteristic surnames. Using the surnames compiled by the first (1790) Census, Thomas Purvis put the percentage of English in the white population at just under 60. Scotch-Irish came in a distant second, at 10 percent, Germans third, at just under 9, and so on, down to Swedes, at 0.3 percent. Forrest and Ellen McDonald, using the same data, found larger numbers of Scots, Irish, and Welsh, particularly in the Southern states, though the English still maintain a hefty national plurality.[9]

These antiquarian exhumations begin to resemble the skull cataloguing of the nineteenth century. The crucial fact is not the blood in the settlers' veins or the shape of their heads, but the cast of their minds. The predominance of ex-Englishmen was more than numerical.

The most obvious manifestation of it was linguistic. There may have been twenty languages in New Netherland, and German survives in Pennsylvania to this day. But the first Americans overwhelmingly thought their thoughts and expressed their conclusions in English. When they looked back, they looked back to Bunyan, Shakespeare, and the King James Bible, not to Luther or Lafontaine. The world is full of fine literary traditions. Only England's happens to be ours.

If English provided the vocabulary, England—specifically, English Whiggery—provided the terms of political discussion. The authority of the Declaration of Independence, wrote Jefferson in his old age, rested on its reflection of the "sentiments of the day, whether expressed in conversation, in letters, printed essays, or in the elementary books of public right, as Aristotle, Cicero, Locke, Sidney, etc."[10] The most important name on this list has traditionally been assumed to be Locke, whose justifications for the Glorious Revolution of 1688 supplied the underpinnings for the American Revolution eighty-seven years later. Debate swirls around this, as around all received opinions. There have been booms in the stock of Locke's younger and more radical contemporaries, John Trenchard and Thomas Gordon, authors of the Cato Letters, and more recently there has been a run on the Scottish philosophers. There have also been arguments over Locke himself: Was he a covert modernist, a rest stop on the highway from Machiavelli to Nietzsche, or was he what he seemed, a moderate whose philosophy fits comfortably with reformed Christianity and natural law?[11] It seems best to accept the traditional view of Locke's importance and his meaning, if only because that is the view the first Americans themselves held. They put him on their shelves and in their heads, and they put him there as a guide to the laws of nature and of nature's God, not as a transvaluator of all values.

The English connection struck many continental observers. Tocqueville, writing sixty years after the Revolution, still spoke of "Anglo-Americans." Santayana, seventy years after Tocqueville, and at the high point of immigration, still wrote of "English liberty in America." Tocqueville was French, and Santayana was born in Madrid and died in Rome, so they can't be accused of grinding Anglo-Saxon axes.

America did not borrow across the board. Large facts of English political experience never impinged here. English liberty in England, Santayana noted, was "crossed and biassed by . . . the church and the aristocracy, entanglement in custom and privilege."[12] Although Edmund Burke got his start in life as an agent for the colony of New York and applauded the American Revolution, his project was almost wholly irrelevant to America's. Whatever conservatives in the English sense there were in the colonies mostly ended up dead, or in Canada. America took from England a language of rights and a certain practice of them, adopted by Dutch burghers, assimilating Mennonites, and Scotch-Irish pioneers alike.

The first Americans brought a third thing in addition to language and liberty from England. But it belongs under the fourth letter.

PROTESTANT

Early America was a country of Protestants. In 1785, out of a total population of about 3 million, there were 24,500 Roman Catholics, white and black, fewer than Quakers, and no more than 3,000 Jews[13]—a tenth of 1 percent of the population.

American Protestants were a certain kind of Protestant. John Updike, interviewed by Henry Bech, "bitterly inveighed against the term Wasp [sic], which implies, he said, Calvinism where he had been Lutheran."[14] This is a real distinction. There were Lutherans in the colonies, as well as Anglicans; both were Protestant churches, hostile to Rome, but emphatic in their retention of hierarchy and sacraments. But most of the English colonists who were religious

professed varieties of Puritanism—Presbyterian, Congregationalist—or faiths further to the ecclesiastic "left"—Baptist, Quaker.
Even the Anglican church in early America was less hierarchical
than it had been at home. Vestries performed many of the functions normally reserved in England for rectors or vicars; there was
no Anglican bishop for the colonies, and rumors that one might be
appointed touched off a political storm in the 1760s. Since many of
the Germans and nearly all of the Dutch and French were Calvinists, the proportion of Americans who fell in or beyond the Reformed band of the Protestant spectrum, by belief or cultural
background, was very high.[15]

What did it mean to be on that end of the spectrum? Among
other things, an emphasis on the inner experience of God's direction. George Fox, English founder of the Society of Friends (he
visited the colonies in the 1670s), described it this way in his *Journal:*
"And when all my hopes" in the church "and in all men were gone,
so that I had nothing outwardly to help me, nor could tell what to
do, then, oh then, I heard a voice which said, 'There is one, even
Christ Jesus, that can speak to thy condition.'"[16] Such events occur
in all Christian literature, from Saul on the road to Damascus to
Dostoyevsky in prison. It is the primary Christian event. What is
striking about the varieties of religious experience that flourished
in America is that they offered little else of equivalent importance—
neither apostolic church nor miraculous sacraments. The signifi-
cance of externalities for low-church Protestants diminishes accor-
dingly. Puritanism, as Perry Miller put it, cast men "on the iron
couch of introspection."[17]

This personal focus had an important social effect: to set America in the direction of religious freedom. Partisans of frontier and
immigrant explanations of America hold that the dispersion of the
population and the diversity of the populace ultimately produced
the First Amendment.[18] But it also mattered what was dispersed.
Calvinists had their flings with theocracy; the Puritans came here to
set one up, and for seventy years they maintained it over most of
New England. Yet it was an inherently unstable enterprise. When it
collapsed, it was as much from squabbles over who could be said to
have had a saving religious experience as from the inexorable
intrusions of non-Puritans. It carried its own doom within it. Other
Reformed Protestants, such as the Baptists, were never so tempted.
Nor could Lockean rights theory alone have produced America's

way with church–state relations. The churches had to want it themselves, and they all came to do so.

It is possible to overstress the religiosity of early America. Then as now, the country went through cycles of rising and falling fervor. The period thirty-five years before the Revolution, the Great Awakening, was a peak. George Whitefield, the English evangelist who barnstormed the colonies, has been called "the first American celebrity."[19] The Revolution and its aftermath were a trough. Several of the founders were Masons or dabblers in other eighteenth century monotheisms. Jefferson wrote a home-made life of Jesus, all morality and no miracles. The percentage of Americans who were actual church members in 1776 has been put at 8 percent. Here, finally, is an effect to which the frontier clearly contributed. Until the invention of the circuit rider, backwoodsmen were obviously beyond the reach of organized religion.

But the reach religion had was strong.* All the important founders respected the religions which surrounded them, even when they adhered to none of them. "All sects here, and we have a great variety," wrote the Deist Franklin of Philadelphia in the last year of his life, "have experienced my goodwill in assisting them with subscriptions for the building their new places of worship."[21] More important, Protestants and ex- or non-Protestants spoke the same language. Jefferson's famous phrase "wall of separation," which has achieved Talmudic status as a commentary on the First Amendment, was written in a letter to a group of Baptists in Danbury, Connecticut. Whatever Jefferson meant, or whatever meanings later exegetes have assigned to him, the Baptists understood him to be engaged with them in a fight for freedom of religions, not from all religion.

The Protestantisms of early America were institutionally and doctrinally divided, but spiritually similar and culturally dominant. These faiths were the faith of the country.

Before we leave the eighteenth century, we have to consider a question raised by the great cataclysm of the nineteenth: Does the South count? It kept up a rebellion for four years, which didn't come from nowhere. Was it radically different all along? Is it still?

All sorts of reasons are adduced to prove the magnitude of the difference. The politics of colonial Virginia, several historians ar-

*In the early 1830s, by way of comparison, Tocqueville observed that Christianity "reigns without obstacle, by universal consent"—even though formal church members, as of 1830, accounted for only 13 percent of the population.[20]

gue, was shaped not by Locke but by his royalist bugaboo, Sir Robert Filmer, who saw society as a family ruled by benign father-kings. Filmer's own family, as it happens, was related to most of the First Families of Virginia.[22] The McDonalds, mentioned earlier, have an ethnic theory of Southern exceptionalism. The Scots, Welsh, and Irish they feel were so heavily represented in the South "took their cultural baggage with them. . . . They were 'indolent to a high degree, unless roused to war, or to any animating amusement.' . . . Politically, they were disputatious and often adroit, but they were inept at governing and nearly impossible to govern."[23] In this view, the last Highland charge was not Culloden, but Gettysburg. Mencken, curiously, agreed. "The chief strain down there, I believe, is Celtic. . . . It not only makes itself visible in physical stigmata—e.g., leanness and dark coloring—but also in mental traits. . . . Every now and then they produce a political leader who puts their notions of the true, the good and the beautiful into plain words, to the amazement and scandal of the rest of the country."[24]

Interesting—to a point. Had the South won, perhaps political independence would have produced a sub-Potomac culture of patriarchs and poets. But South and North have been yoked for more than a century since the Civil War, after having been yoked for almost a century before it. The man who larded the Declaration of Independence with Locke was a Virginian. The pressure of extreme historical stress, such as that generated by a revolution, can catalyze a character type. When a revolution fails, as the South's failed, the type dies aborning. The South was different enough to break away, not different enough to stay away. It makes more sense to consider the undeniable differences between North and South as the result of variations within an original American type, not of separate types.

Time now to abandon such words and phrases as early Americans, colonial Americans, founders, settlers. What we have pieced together is the WASP, and WASPs pieced together America. Other people might have done it instead, or prevented its being done: The Indians might have won a few more battles, the slaves could have revolted, France might have pushed Quebec all the way to the Delaware River. But white English Protestants preempted them. Time now to examine their character.

3
★
The Way of the WASP

WHEN BENJAMIN FRANKLIN decided to improve his own character, he drew up the list of virtues which so annoyed D. H. Lawrence. Originally there were twelve. "But a Quaker friend having kindly informed me that I was generally thought proud . . . of which he convinced me by mentioning several instances; I determined endeavoring to cure myself, if I could, of this vice or folly among the rest, and I added *Humility* to my list"—along with an explanatory note: "Imitate Jesus and Socrates."[1]

Virtues, which we hope to acquire, may be listed. Character, which is what we are, is more complex. The basic WASP character can be broken down into six traits, which may be arranged in the following mantra. Traits form pairs and connections across the pattern, as well as between neighbors.

Conscience

Antisensuality   Industry

Use   Success

Civic-mindedness

Let us take the traits in order, starting at noon.

Conscience. Conscience is the great legacy of P. It is the way WASPs regulate their inner life and monitor their behavior. You let

your conscience be your guide. It guides by offering a clear vision of
the way you should go. The way may be spelled out in law or scripture,
but conscience is the window through which each man comes to see it.
All WASPs, not just Quakers, believe in the inner light.

Sight is the sense of conscience. George Fox in his perplexity
heard a voice, and so did the born-again Englishman John Newton.

Amazing Grace! How sweet the *sound* . . .

Yet after the first rearranging experience, sight and insight take
over the management of life.

I once was lost but now am found,
Was blind, but now I *see.*

This was the WASP's point of contact with the Enlightenment and
its self-evident (evident = completely seen) truths. This was also
what Emerson, that subtle renegade, appropriated for his own
project. "Standing on bare ground—my head bathed by the blithe
air and uplifted into infinite space. . . . I become a transparent
eyeball; I am nothing; I see all . . . "[2]

The way that conscience sees must be plain, or else what good is it
for guidance? The way that can be seen is not the way, said Lao Tzu,
but the way that cannot be seen is not the way of the WASP. Paradox
and ambiguity are distractions, if not worse. The path is straight as
well as plain. Byways lead to waste and confusion, if not actual Hell.

The punishment for ignoring the guidance of conscience is ad-
ministered by conscience itself, in the form of guilt. Guilt, like
conscience, is a private matter, inward and individual. No amount
of external opprobrium can increase or enlarge it. It is a very
different thing from shame. Shame is embarrassment before someone else—parents, friends, community. It is publicly displayed by
the blush. Guilt is a pang. If it shows itself to the world, as in the
mark that appears finally on the Reverend Arthur Dimmesdale's
breast, it is only after long internal gnawing and a conscious act of
self-exposure by the guilty party. Shame, being a public transac-
tion, is a two-way street. It may be induced by peers or betters. The
conviction of guilt is always *in camera.*

Wherever societies are small, tight, and stable, approaching the
condition of oyster beds or coral reefs—peasant societies the world
over—shame is the preferred method of discipline. WASPs believe
in guilt, which travels anywhere.

This is why conscience is the most effective monitor of behavior
ever devised. It doesn't quit when the oracles fall silent or when the

cops go off duty. In societies ruled by conscience, people stop for red lights at three o'clock in the morning. In societies with less alert monitors, people drive on the sidewalk.

Conscience is the source of whatever freedoms WASP society enjoys. Since all consciences have an equally clear view of truth, who could presume to meddle with any man's? But conscience also limits freedom, which becomes the freedom to do what you know you should do. "Confirm thy soul in self-control,/Thy liberty in [moral] law."

Industry. One of the things conscience directs you to do is work. Idle hands do the Devil's. "The hours have wings," wrote John Milton, "and fly up to the Author of Time with reports on how we have used them"—a sentiment I first read not for some English major's project, but as a little boy in an advice column by Billy Graham that ran in the innermost pages of the local paper. I usually didn't read Graham, but this struck me as a bull's-eye. What could be more obvious?

Busy-ness suggests business, which suggests in turn Max Weber's proposition that Protestantism, especially in its Calvinist forms, is the engine of work in the Western world. Sociologists have recently found that the economic gap between white Protestants and white Catholics in this country has vanished, which means, however, not that Catholicism has suddenly become hospitable to work, but that American Catholics have Americanized (Protestantized) themselves. John Cuddihy, in his elegant encapsulation of Weber, hints that Protestant industry is a kind of nervous ritual, almost a reaction formation: "To rid themselves of this intolerable uncertainty"—predestination—Calvinists "reassured themselves by creating capitalism."[3] Whatever the dynamic, you must be doing things. Contemplation—the mystic's way, or the hermit's—is not an option.

Industry devalues all forms of prestige that rest on other criteria. So much for aristocracy. George Bush, graduating from college, went to Texas rather than Brown Brothers, Harriman, to make his nut (though he would use money raised through friends and relatives back east). One of Herbert Hoover's cousins once asked their grandmother if it was true that they were related to John Wesley, and got the following response: "What matter if we descended from the highest unless we are something ourselves? Get busy."[4]

Success. The reward of industry is success, which WASPs admire extravagantly. In theological terms, success is the outward and visible sign of grace—Cuddihy's "reassurance." By your works you know yourself. It is ironic, of course, that a religious impulse that began with a rejection of the doctrine of salvation by works should end in a glorification of the results of work. But the mere fact that WASPs distrust paradoxes does not mean they are immune to them.

An obvious measure of success is cash. Yet there are times when the only success that has been achieved is internal—when an effort or an exertion that has been good for nothing else has been good for you. The maxim that is commonly, but wrongly, attributed to Vince Lombardi—"Winning isn't everything, it's the only thing"—is a case of getting it not quite right. The climactic football game in *Stover at Yale* is a defeat; the heroes don't even manage to score. What Dink Stover learns from the experience is to take his lumps without complaining. Which leads him to later triumphs, of course.

What Lombardi actually said was that "winning isn't everything; wanting to win is." Is this any better? Success follows industry, yet the motivational spark between the two is problematic. James Madison, in one of the most famous Federalist papers, put ambition at the center of the constitutional system. But he handled the subject with the care—and distaste—of a lab technician preparing inoculations. "Ambition," he wrote, "must be made to counteract ambition. It may be a reflection on human nature," he went on, "that such devices should be necessary to control the abuses of government. But what is government itself but the greatest of all reflections on human nature?"[5] Only our depravity forces us to consider such depraved subjects. This was the aspect of WASPhood, facsimile and authentic, which the young Norman Podhoretz found hardest to bear: "the hunger for worldly success was regarded as low, ignoble, ugly . . . something to be ashamed of and guilty about. My own conversion to such values" marked "the first lap in the long, blind journey I was making."[6]

The English who stayed home are also suspicious of ambition, but the social origin of their leeriness is rather different—an emulation of the attitudes of an aristocracy, which does not yearn to win because it has, by definition of birth, won already. Hoover's grandmother would have been appalled. What the WASP wants is to follow the work conscience lays out. Success, public or personal, will come in the nature of things. But that is the operation of providential or natural laws. The credit is Providence's, or Nature's. Meanwhile, "'Tis not in mortals to command success," says a character in Addison's *Cato*, George Washington's favorite play. "But we'll do more, Sempronius; we'll deserve it."[7]

Industry and success together explain why America, whose original colonial economy—tobacco and pelts—was strictly Third World, a page out of Lenin, became, in three centuries, the largest economy on the globe. Economists make the point continually, but it has to be stated again, because people forget it continually: America didn't get rich because it had "natural resources." Plenty of places on earth have them in equal or greater measure. Americans did well for themselves because of their moral resources—the obligations of industry and the respect they accorded success.

Civic-mindedness. WASPs pay lip service, and often even service, to the good of society as a whole. All other social facts—honor, family, group—take a back seat.

Consider the rarity in WASP America of duels, feuds, and secret societies, all expressions of loyalties to subcivic ideals. Alexander Hamilton died in a duel, but he opposed the practice, and religious opposition stamped it out in the early nineteenth century. Feuds occur only in the boondocks. The Masons, after provoking the first third party in American history, the Anti-Masonic Party, became like Ralph Kramden's Racoon Lodge. Skull and Bones, Dink Stover's secret college society—and George Bush's—justified itself by its social usefulness. "It makes fellows get out and work . . . and keeps a pretty good, clean, temperate atmosphere about the place."[8]

WASP defenders of capitalism also make their case in civic terms. The rising tide lifts all boats. *Atlas Shrugged,* a bald sermon on love of self, sells thousands of copies to teenage girls every year. But Ayn Rand's pitch—like Lombardi's—is slightly off. Among WASPs, free enterprise preens itself on what it does for everybody, not just for supermen. Without civic-mindedness, the successful would have no sense of social responsibility. They often have little enough. But thanks to civic-mindedness—the operation of conscience in social relations—they have some. Even Social Darwinism in its most naked form, which enjoyed a vogue at the end of the nineteenth century, promised, by casting aside the unfit, to benefit society as a whole in the long run.

Special interests have been the demons of American political rhetoric from the days of the Populists until now. Madison called them factions—parts, less than the whole, mobilized for advantage or gain. Realistically, he knew they would emerge. But he devised a system to blunt their effectiveness, which he expected the country to possess sufficient civic virtue to maintain. In politics, the charge of representing special interests, if true, is indefensible. The only recourse is to accuse the accuser of defending worse ones.

WASPs have long been fascinated with tales of groups that are hierarchical, secret, self-interested (in short, criminal): Jesuits, the Mafia, Bloods and Crips. It is a fascination with the foreign. Equally popular are tales of the loner—the vigilante, the private eye, the gunslinger—who, when society reneges on its responsibilities, takes the law into his own hands. Pretty clearly, these are daydreams of people who do not often do likewise.

Civic society exercises discipline not so much by the force of law—people may not break the law very often; if the laws are plain, why should they?—as by conformity. The relentless conformism of WASP life seems to negate the primacy of conscience, and many books have become cocktail chatter by plying the apparent contradictions: inner-direction vs. other-direction, Consciousness I vs. Consciousness II. The contradictions vanish with a little thought. Even if conscience is our guide, only a handful of eccentrics—half geniuses, half lunatic—are ever able to live completely from their own resources at all times. A normal man requires the additional support of some authority in many of the occasions of his life. What will the authority be? the past? the gods? the police? Or the example of his peers, each one of whom, after all, bears a conscience akin to his own? WASPs, when they must obey, choose to obey each other. They are encouraged in conformity by the additional fact that since the insights of conscience are plain, men's consciences will tend naturally to follow a similar course. "Each sect" in America, wrote Toqueville, "adores the Deity in its own peculiar manner, but all sects preach the same moral law."[9]

The pressure of conformity, finally, ensures that crackpots—who may be prophets—must pass the test of time. Conformity's enemies accuse it of muzzling invention, of keeping Miltons mute and inglorious. But it also inhibits charlatans and maniacs. Genuine contributions to the common weal, WASPs believe, will always make their way.

Use. We have encountered use, or usefulness, before in other points of the pattern—the usefulness of work, the usefulness of capitalism. But it is important enough to be given a portion to itself. For nothing is ever good, the WASP believes, simply and of itself. It must be good for something.

A good use of something is the fulfillment of its proper task. WASPs like to think of themselves as handy: with wrenches and committees, assembly lines and constitutions. They like getting the job done, and they enjoy contemplating "last things, fruits, consequences, facts."[10] Inefficiency is the practical equivalent of ambiguity—a kind of sin. H. G. Wells, in one of his novels, shows the secretary of the Massachusetts Society for the Study of Contemporary Thought reacting to the contrary habits of an English country house. "The point that strikes me most about all this is that that barn isn't a barn any longer, and that this farmyard isn't a farmyard. There isn't any wheat or chaff or anything of that sort in the barn, and there never will be again: there's just a pianola and a dancing floor, and if a cow came into this farmyard, everybody in the place would be shooing it out again."[11]

Use affects the WASP's attitude to time. The self-improving Franklin, believing that "the precept of *Order* requir[ed] that *every part of my business should have its allotted time*," devised the following plan for his day.

THE MORNING		
Question. What good shall I do this day?	5	Rise, wash, and address
	6	*Powerful Goodness!* Contrive
	7	day's business, and take the resolution of the day; prosecute the present study, and breakfast.
	8	
	9	Work
	10	
	11	
NOON	12	Read, or overlook my accounts, and dine.
	1	
	2	
	3	Work
	4	
	5	
EVENING	6	Put things in their places.
Question. What good have I done today?	7	Supper. Music or diversion,
	8	or conversation. Examination of the day.
	9	
	10	
	11	
	12	
NIGHT	1	Sleep
	2	
	3	
	4	

("I found myself," he added ruefully, "incorrigible with respect to order.")[12] Time is the tyrant of daily life; it must be obeyed, and more than obeyed. To arrive anywhere only on time is to arrive late.

Use also molds the WASP's view of time past. Despite the Bicentennial Tall Ships, colonial Williamsburg, and a hundred other restorations, authentic and fake, the WASP's attitude to his own history is nostalgic, wistful, curious—but not intimate. (The Civil War may be the lone exception.) To his European prehistory he has even less connection. History washed overboard into the Atlantic. In Dublin, a speaker can draw a crowd in midweek, in business hours, by talking about Wolfe Tone. As recently as seventy years ago, Michael Dukakis's cousins were trying to undo the fall of Constantinople. These events might have happened yesterday. In men's minds, they're still happening today. The WASP mind asks irritably, What good does it do me, now? "The only history worth a tinker's dam," wrote Henry Ford, "is the history we make today."[13] Important history flunks the test of time, but so do grudges and festering hatreds.

Antisensuality. Every other point of the pattern is some positive thing or quality. Here we resort to the negative. What is negated is any keen attachment to pleasures that operate through the senses. No single positive term quite covers all cases. The suggestion of vigilant guardedness makes the negative doubly appropriate.

We should not exaggerate. The WASP is not a crazed oppressor of the body, no anchorite, no saddhu. Sports of all kinds have always been important to him. WASPs race horses and cars, and blast away at birds; they invented baseball, basketball, and football, and took up polo (those who could afford it) with enthusiasm. Yet sports are always, inescapably, good for you. They build your muscles and your character. ("How did your *team* do, dear?"). They may yield spiritual gratifications like success, but not sensual ones. The body is to be exercised, not pleased.

So it goes, through everything men enjoy. Consider the plainness of WASP food. Not that most non-WASP Americans have anything to boast about in this regard. An immigrant pool drawn largely from Ireland, Germany, and Eastern Europe was not calculated to improve the national cuisine. (Just what America needed—five hundred kinds of starch.) One of the mysteries of American life is how the injection of millions of Italians could have failed utterly to raise the general level. It is the same with drink as with food. WASPs drink to get drunk. The only alternative to drunkenness is temperance. The care the French, Italians, and Germans take over wine, or even the English over beer and ale, is incomprehensible to them.

WASPs break the Seventh Commandment as often as anybody else. But mistresses, as an established aristocratic or *haut-bourgeois* institution, are as rare as spice racks. Transgressors show indecent disrespect for the opinion of mankind. The best posthumous defense Richard Harding Davis could make for his friend Stanford White, who had been murdered by a former lover's husband, was that the dead man got a lot of exercise outside the bedroom. "Described as a voluptuary, his greatest pleasure was to stand all day waist deep in the rapids of a Canadian river and fight it out with a salmon."[14] The ground has shifted on sex, but old habits die hard. What was forbidden becomes compulsory. The real subject of *The Joy of Sex*, as its National Lampoon parodists realized, was *The Job of Sex*.[15]

The arts too are a job. WASPs are great consumers of culture even if, as we shall see, they are burdened and ambivalent producers of it. But the pleasure they take is inevitably alloyed with self-improvement—among the sincere, that is. Among the insincere, the pleasure comes from the joys of status. To be on "speaking terms" with "fine things," observed Santayana, "was a part of social respectability, like those candlesticks, probably candleless, sometimes displayed as a seemly ornament in a room blazing with electric light."[16]

Antisensuality serves the practical function of limiting the enjoyment of success, at least of unearned success. Plantation owners did not live austerely, and neither did robber barons. But they could all claim to have done something, even if it was only assembling a trust. For WASPs, all rewards exist on sufferance; rewards that are simply inherited excite suspicion. "A great fortune had been entrusted to him," one of Trollope's characters says of the Duke of Omnium, "and he knew that it was his duty to spend it. He did spend it, and all the world looked up to him."[17] Not the WASP world. Antisensuality threatens the lazy rich with a bad conscience. And so we come back to noon.

WASPs have no monopoly on any one of these traits: Chinese work hard; Jews know something about guilt. But the combination of all of them, and the way they temper and modify each other—success depending on industry; use giving industry its tasks; civic-mindedness placing obligations on success, and antisensuality setting limits to the enjoyment of it; conscience watching over everything—is uniquely WASP. The way of the WASP was shaped by the same forces that shaped him. English notions of liberty and society molded his notions of civic-mindedness. WASP Protestantism generated WASP ideas about work, success, and sensuality. Both helped establish the primacy of conscience, with Protestantism playing the larger role. Any change in the shaping forces, or in any of the traits themselves, would change the WASP's character.

The way of the WASP can lead in a number of different directions and take a variety of social forms. WASPs can be, and have been, imperialists and America firsters, followers of Social Darwinism and of prairie socialism. For more than eighty years, the country they built was half slave and half free. Yet certain social structures, some good, most monstrous—fascism, communism, the caste system—are out of bounds. Everything that is within bounds will be done in the characteristic behavioral style.

The way of the WASP can also lead to frustrations. We shall be examining some of these later on, but not plain crime and sin. Millions of WASPs have committed every imaginable un-WASPy act, from coming to the theater after the curtain goes up to coveting other mens' wives. This is disobedience, not deviance. All thieves support the institution of property; they are simply original in their way of acquiring it. The way of the WASP may be shaken by revolt or weakened by defection, but, like any other way, it withstands ordinary failure.

Two other forms of disobedience, or at least relaxation, are humor and fun (as in *good, clean*). Bergson thought laughs were human barks, a means of warning and social control, a conservative force. But they are also an outlet, an underside. WASP humor, like all humor, conceals many a tiny rebellion. In its occasional savagery there is revolt against as well as expression of conscience's grip. Fun, meanwhile, operates as a distraction. It fools the radar of conscience and allows the WASP to enjoy activities—music, for instance—without confronting the potentially serious counterclaims they make against his way. Fun is the Stealth technology of the psyche.

But the most important thing the way of the WASP has led to is American peace and prosperity. It explains why we are richer than

Russia, though we have fewer natural resources; calmer than Lebanon, though we have more sects; freer and more just than either. It also explains why so many Russians and Lebanese, and people of numerous other societies, have come here.

4

✫

Others, and the WASP World They Aspired To

*I*N ITS BRIEF HISTORY, America has experienced the greatest population transfer the Western world has known since the fall of Rome, with happier results.

This human tsunami has been seen as a simple transfer, not an amalgamation: a shift of bodies, not souls. Michael Novak called ethnics unmeltable. Father Andrew Greeley, the novelist and pollster, pops up every few years with a study showing how different Catholic and Protestant Americans continue to be (and justifying, incidentally, the existence of priestly pollsters).

Many WASPs have made similar assumptions about the tenacity of immigrant behavior and have brooded about the effects it would have on their way. "It is an axiom," Captain John B. Trevor, a lobbyist for restricted immigration, warned Congress in 1924, "that government not imposed by external force is the visible expression of the ideals, standards, and social viewpoint of the people over which it rules." Trevor got his rank in military intelligence, for which he had monitored the activities of radical groups in New York after World War I, an experience that made him suspicious of the people America had recently been getting. "The races [sic] from southern and eastern Europe . . . cannot point during a period of seven centuries since Magna Charta to any conception of successful government other than a paternal autocracy." Trevor's first sentence was no fallacy, it was pure Tocqueville; and though one could quarrel with "paternal autocracy" in the second, one could not challenge the larger point: that, whatever form government took in the old countries of Southern and Eastern Europe, from city state to *shtetl,* it did not have a lot to do with the Magna Carta. "If, therefore," Trevor concluded, "the principle of individual liberty guarded by constitutional government"—the way of the WASP—"is to endure, the basic strain of our population must be maintained."[1] So sell the Statue of Liberty for scrap.

But Trevor's conclusion does not necessarily follow from his premises. The trouble with his fears, and with ethnic pride, is that they both underestimate the psychological rupture of immigration. The leap from an old country that any immigrant makes is sundering. The new country confronts him with new ideals, standards, and social viewpoints. Under any circumstances, the pressure of the new ideals and standards will be compelling. If they happen to be, in crucial respects, superior to the immigrants' old ones, the attraction will be doubly powerful.

Immigrants have brought thousands of things here, in their baggage or in their minds, from snacks to religions. What none of them has successfully established is a rival way of life. For most of the history of American immigration, the dock or the tarmac was the first step in becoming WASPs.

The others—who are by now the vast majority of Americans— came in four great swells, each composed of smaller distinct currents.

Germans and Irish—Irish-Irish, in addition to Scotch-Irish— began arriving in colonial times, hit a peak with the famines and revolutions of the 1840s, and continued at that level for some decades. In the last third of the century they were joined, then surpassed, by people from every other country of Europe, from Portugal to Finland. This wave, interrupted by World War I, was virtually halted by the immigration laws of the 1920s that Captain Trevor was so keen to pass. The West Coast experienced its own influx of Chinese and Japanese earlier, beginning with the Gold Rush and ending with earlier restrictive acts. In 1965, after a forty-year lull, the gates opened again. Attorney General Robert Kennedy, testifying before Congress in 1964, expected five thousand immigrants from the "Asia-Pacific triangle" in the first year of the proposed law, "after which immigration from that source would virtually disappear."[2] The attorney general was mistaken. The last twenty-five years have seen a rush of newcomers, legal and illegal, from the triangle, as well as from Latin America and the Caribbean, from West Africa, and from some oldtime spots of Europe—Ireland, Russia—that were getting a second wind. A New Yorker buys his fruit from Koreans, his newspapers from Indians, and his umbrellas, when he is caught on Fifth Avenue without one, from Senegalese peddlers. Knowing that Senegal was a former French colony, the police in the early eighties assigned a francophone cop to deal with the peddlers, only to discover that the only language they spoke was the African tongue Wolof. The social service ads in the subways, more savvily, assure Haitians *nou pale kreyol.* When Washingtonians tire of Vietnamese restaurants, they go to Afghan ones. (Lose a country, gain a cuisine.) Cinco de Mayo is a holiday in South Texas, the Bay of Pigs is a day of infamy in Miami. One of the last places on earth where Aramaic, the language of Jesus, is used is Hackensack, New Jersey. The experiences of at least the European immigrants of the first two waves have been thoroughly, in some cases obsessively, recorded. The third wave is sure to get similar treatment. To these must be added the journeying of American blacks, in two stages, one compulsory, one internal: the slave trade, which lasted from the early seventeenth century to 1808; then, beginning in the 1920s, the migration of blacks from south to north, sucked like leaves by the furnace of industry.

Some of these groups of others slid into WASPhood with remarkably little trouble. The first and largest European immigrant group, the Germans, showed an extreme of docility. Though they did not speak the language, and though they had certain unWASPy habits—they drank regularly and to moderation, and they knew something about music—they fitted in without much ado. It has been suggested that this happened because they were such a heterogeneous lot to begin with—farmers and city folk, laborers and intelligentsia, Protestants, Catholics, and Jews. "They reflected," Nathan Glazer and Daniel Moynihan wrote, "an entire modern society, not simply an element of one."[3] They maintained numerous parallel institutions—churches, schools, newspapers (twenty-seven German-language dailies by 1860). But when in this century America twice fought Germany, the Germans simply closed the parallel institutions down. Many anglicized their names. Many had already done so—Dink Stover's parents or grandparents had probably spelled it Stouffer.

Other groups had serious problems of adjustment, though they managed to keep them to themselves. The Sicilians in America, wrote Luigi Barzini, the Milanese journalist who lived here for five years in the twenties, "as they had done since the days of Homer, neatly divided human beings into friends, enemies, and neutrals. Their rule (which is also a Spanish proverb) was 'To friends, everything; to enemies, the law.' . . . The family and its allies then became a Macedonian phalanx going through American society as if through butter."[4] In the service of their families, Italians reimmigrated in larger numbers than any other group. Though more than 2 million Italians arrived here in the first decade of the twentieth century, the 1910 census counted scarcely more than a million in the country. The reason was that as soon as they had made some money, most of the new arrivals promptly sent it, and themselves, back to the home folks. Yet this intense—and, in the WASP world, inordinate—family loyalty, except when it was turned to crime, had no negative social effects (except, it may be, on Italians themselves). The Italians who settled down here lived peaceably with non-Italian neighbors: Jews and Chinese in New York, blacks in Louisiana. Howard Beach and Bensonhurst were headlines in the eighties, but they are historical anomalies. Italians have shown only moderate skill in running ethnic political machines, and scant interest in home country politics. The Italians' intense involvement in their families violated the imperative of civic-mindedness, but it permitted a passive conformity with other WASP ways.

But for some groups of others, fitting into the WASP world was a process fraught with turmoil. The experience of the Irish—not the dour Orange garrison of Ulster, but the Irish the word usually conjures up—offers an extreme case of the difficulties of blending in, and of success even in spite of difficulties.

To other newcomers, the Irish seem at a distance to be WASPs. Novak excluded them from his book on the grounds that they were not ethnic enough. To American Catholics from Eastern Europe, he noted, any parish without a national prefix—Polish, Slovak, whatever—was assumed to be Irish. The Irish, in other words, needed no arrivals' identifier; they were established. "The nuances of the regional Irish-Yankee feud [in Boston] escaped Brad" Schaeffer, a character in an Updike story, "since to his Midwestern eyes the two inimical camps were very similar—thin-skinned, clubby men from damp green islands, fond of a nip and long malicious stories."[5]

The perception of congruence was based on powerful WASP-Irish similarities. The Irish knew the language. They were familiar with the English half of Anglo-American liberties, even if only by being deprived of them. Temperamentally, they made an excellent fit with certain aspects of the way of the WASP. The Irish are even more puritanical than the Puritans. "I inclined his young mind," a character in *Molloy* says of his son, "towards that most fruitful of dispositions, horror of the body and its functions."[6] The Irish handle drink in the same way as WASPs: alcoholism or teetotaling.

Yet the Irish record in America is filled with problems. In terms of average income, the Irish advanced slowly relative to later immigrant groups. The Irish ran urban and statewide political machines, a sign of power but also of parochialism and segregation. Many of the pathologies associated with the crackheads and AFDC familes of today were rife in the Irish slums of the early nineteenth century; the worst riot in American history, the New York City draft riot of 1863, which left nearly a thousand people dead, was an Irish outbreak against a system of conscription that oppressed them.

These are statistics and headlines; symptoms, not causes. The source of Irish difficulties—difficulties experienced, to some degree, by many newcoming others—was a fundamental problem they had with the way of the WASP.

For years the Irish maintained a dual political loyalty, a consuming interest in the affairs of another country. In 1870 a private army of Irishmen attacked Canada from Vermont. Twelve decades later, aged bomb-throwers still march in St. Patrick's Day parades. The meddling in Irish and British politics is now mostly ritual, but sentiments of grievance against the former oppressor, difficult for a WASP to credit, remain. "The Irish," as John Roche puts it, "wear bandages to remind themselves where their wounds were."[7]

They also indulged in intergroup vendettas here. Their partners in uproar until they disappeared as an identifiable ethnic group were the Scotch-Irish. Green-Orange riots and brawls regularly accompanied celebrations of St. Patrick's Day and the Battle of Boyne in the nineteenth century. The Irish also picked fights with non-Irish immigrant groups among whom they lived—Jews, blacks, Germans, Chinese, Italians. "How did you know they were wops when you bumped them off?" a bit character in *In Our Time* asks another, who has just murdered two Hungarians. "Wops," answers the killer, whose name is Boyle, "I can tell wops a mile off."[8]

All this indicates a deficiency in the cardinal WASP public virtue, civic mindedness. In its place the Irish showed clan-mindedness. It was based, in part, on a plausible suspicion of the justice of any social system, fostered by their experience in Ireland. But it persisted long after they had left Ireland behind. The Irish wished to, and did, escape in the flesh. The escape of the mind was more difficult.

What about the keystone of the WASP's private life—conscience? The keeper of Irish conscience was, until quite recently, the Roman Catholic Church. For a century the Irish ruled it, and it ruled them. One of the French clerics who still ran the American church at the end of the eighteenth century referred to the Irish members of his flock as *canaille*. By the end of the nineteenth century, their grip on its institutions and hierarchy was so strong that non-Irish American Catholics complained all the way to Rome.

Many WASPs doubted, and some loudly denied, that large numbers of newcomers, obedient to an institution that was so much older than the United States, and so inimical, as it seemed, to republican government, could live in peace here. It is one of the pleasant surprises of the Irish experience that Catholicism adapted so well. The reason is plain. The Catholic Church in America became Americanized—that is, WASPized. The Catholic Church arrived as the one true faith, outside which there was no salvation, and it became a denomination. It was still the one true faith, of course, but then so were all the others. It never pushed its claims politically, and it learned to be polite about pushing its claims polemically. When a WASP controversialist challenged Al Smith, on the eve of the 1928 election, to affirm or reject the triumphalist implications of certain papal encyclicals, Smith is said to have asked his advisers, "Will someone tell me what the hell a papal encyclical is?"[9] Quoted out of context, it reads like a joke on Smith's ignorance of theology. Properly understood, it is a sad, almost tragic joke on the completeness of Irish Catholicism's assimilation. Will someone tell me, Smith was asking, what the hell a papal encyclical that is contrary to the spirit of American politics *could be*? Such a thing, he assumed in the strength of his faith—his double faith: in his church, and in the ways of his country—could not exist. The church of the Irish quickly acquired an attitude toward public expressions of conscience indistinguishable from that of its suspicious neighbors.

The domestication of the Irish Catholic Church is important, because it shows how assimilation works. Others do not assimilate to the way of the WASP by learning the language or getting a job, though these are important. The process is more than a matter of recognizing that life here is better than it was at home. The immigrant knew that when he arrived, sometimes before he arrived. Assimilation occurs when the outsider intuits the character traits that *make* life here better for him. "One man prefers the Republic," Mencken remarked, "because it pays better wages than Bulgaria. . . . Another because there is a warrant out for him somewhere else."[10] As usual, Mencken is jeering. But drain away the spleen, and it turns out that he is talking about economic opportunity and political freedom. Internal assimilation—the only important kind—occurs when the job seeker and the refugee understand, intellectually or unconsciously, why the way of the WASP leads to higher wages and fewer warrants. For Irish and other Catholics, America offered something almost unknown in the post-Reformation history of their church: a country, filled with non-Catholics, which placed no penalties on the faithful. They immediately saw that this was better than being persecuted; they came to see, based on the enormous strides their church made—by 1850, it was the largest in America, a position it has held to this day—that WASP ideals of conscience and civic-mindedness were even preferable to those of societies in which Catholics themselves ruled and persecuted. Once they saw that, they were well on the way to becoming the only kind of WASP that counts: WASPs by conviction.

The Roman Catholic Church was the one immigrant institution which had the numbers, the force of tradition, and the intellectual weight to have deflected the American character, or at least split it. The fact that it did not, and that good Catholics became good Americans, which is to say, good WASPs, is the most dramatic proof of the gravitational power of the WASP world.

Literal WASPs were not passive spectators of these assorted perplexities and achievements. They involved themselves directly in their neighbors' affairs and experienced strong reactions to their presence. The involvement and the reactions fell, unsurprisingly, into two broad categories: hostile and welcoming. For half a century the hostility became so rancorous that many WASPs slid into clan-mindedness, behaving like any other imperfectly adjusted ethnic group.

Hostility was as old as immigration. The second American third party, after the Anti-Masons, was the Know-Nothings, or the American party. Its enemies were the Irish, and it distrusted them because of their combination of Catholicism and political skill. The

Know-Nothings swelled and burst in a matter of years; their one presidential candidate, the hapless Millard Fillmore, who rejected their program, carried only one state in 1856. But anti-Catholicism lingered on—lingers today. Jimmy Swaggart assured his viewers in the 1980s that all Mother Teresa's care for beggars wouldn't keep her out of Hell.

The long and various second wave (which coincided with the Irish assumptions of control over the big-city machines they had formerly supported) became the occasion for more complicated hostilities. Anti-Semitism appeared in American life in the 1870s. The phenomenon was sudden, unprecedented, and sometimes ironic in its workings. Digby Baltzell tells the story of Jesse Seligman, a founder of the Union League Club, one of the stuffiest upper-crust preserves in New York, who resigned his membership in 1893 when his own son was blackballed.[11] The South, which had enjoyed a false dawn of legal racial equality under Reconstruction and under the Democratic grandees who took over when the Federal troops left, began imposing Jim Crow in the 1880s and 1890s. All these strains—anti-Catholic, anti-Jewish, antiblack—were brought together in the second Ku Klux Klan of the 1920s, which, unlike its predecessor and its successors, was neither an all-Southern group nor a fringe of lowlifes and skinheads, but a national organization with strength in the North and the Midwest. At the Democratic convention of 1924, a pro-Klan candidate hung in the race through one hundred ballots.

Feelings of WASP dislike and dismay were not confined to troglodytes. Jokes about Irishmen and their boggy feet disfigure *Walden*. Genteel urban reformers were as alarmed as the Invisible Empire by the foreignness of their opponents. One of Margaret Sanger's motives in campaigning for birth control was to limit the breeding of lesser breeds. Madison Grant, a founder of the New York Zoological Society and the Save the Redwoods League, was author of *The Passing of the Great Race in America,* an anti-immigration scare book which Jay Gatsby's Long Island neighbor, Tom Buchanan, seems to have read.

More than motiveless malignity lay behind these reactions. We have already examined the political argument against taking in large numbers of others—John Trevor's. WASPs also feared economic competition from transplanted businessmen at the top and from toiling masses below. Immigrants, as the Imperial Wizard of the twenties Klan put it, "fill the lower rungs of the ladder of success." This is, in the aggregate, a fallacy—new labor floats an economy, it does not sink it—though there will always be individuals displaced by those who work harder and better or who hold lower expectations. WASPs were not the only ones who feared displacement. At the height of the second wave, the United Garment Workers of America, no WASP coterie, deplored "the overstocking of the labour market" with those "unfitted to battle intelligently for their rights." Last one in raise the drawbridge.[12]

There was, finally, a sense among WASPs that the psychological burden of assimilation did not lie only on the assimilating. The melters had difficulties of which the melted were unaware. Tolerance, a writer in the *Christian Century* pointed out in 1945, twenty years after the second wave had been halted, "is chiefly Protestant tolerance. Whatever degree of tolerance (if any) [that] is produced in the other groups is hardly more than academic and sentimental, because, being a minority, they have no concrete occasion to exercise it."[13] One can almost see the wan smile of the host who was happy, at eight o'clock, to throw a party, but who, at two in the morning, with the guests still filling his sofa and the ring marks multiplying on his tables, is less happy.

One effect of these hostilities, and the lack of confidence they betoken, was to create in many WASPs, from the 1880s to the 1920s, an ethnic consciousness, with all its attendant problems. Clubs, schools, and political movements became preoccupied with "stock," as if they were dealing with horses rather than humans. There even developed a dual loyalty among many WASPs to England: the Anglo-Saxon fad. George Apley wrote during World War I of "our former Mother Country . . . saving civilization for posterity,"[14] and let his daughter be wooed by a con man posing as an English officer.

Hostility continually recurs, and is therefore important. Equally important is its recurring shallowness. WASP ethnicity was an episode. So were other manifestations of clannishness. We have already noted the brief and inglorious history of the Know-Nothings. The Democratic party the Klan fought to control seventy years later was a minority party, and the Klan lost the fight. Immigration from Southern and Eastern Europe was restricted for only forty-one years; Japanese and Chinese immigrants were blocked for only decades more. Every acrid reference in WASP letters or diaries to "alien vermin" swarming out of "steerage" can be matched by a paean: "the inner light of Pilgrim and Quaker colonists . . . gleams no less in the faces of the children of Russian Jew immigrants today."[15]

The large fact, larger than exclusion, is that non-WASPs were welcome—welcome enough, anyway, that most of them stayed, and more kept coming. The practical motives for WASP hospitality were supplied by industry and use. A country so big and booming needed people. The magnates who, as clubmen, blackballed the Seligmans of the world profited, as businessmen, from the immigration of their cousins. The treatment accorded newcomers once they arrived was dictated, for the most part, by civic-mindedness. The liberties WASPs had devised for themselves applied to everyone. By itself, Bartholdi's statue, "Liberty Enlightening the World," is Gallic and abstract. In New York Harbor, a stone's throw from Ellis Island, where the world flowed in beneath it, it expressed an American reality.

The exception, the special case, as always, is blacks, slaves for two centuries, second-class citizens for a century more. To which one can only say that the war which emancipated them was not nothing; neither is the money that has been spent on the black poor in the last twenty-five years. Whether it has been spent to anyone's benefit is another matter.

The only price even the most inclusive WASPs exacted was that newly arrived others should become exactly like themselves. Theodore Roosevelt, in the thick of the immigration debates sparked by the second wave, put it most simply. Roosevelt accepted the economic argument against unrestricted inflow, and he also believed there was such a thing as "races [sic again] which do not readily assimilate with our own." Against the sweep of his premises, these reservations shrink to cavils. "Where immigrants, or the sons of immigrants, do not heartily and in good faith throw in their lot with us, but cling to the speech, the customs, the ways of life, and the habits of thought of the Old World which they have left, they thereby do harm both to themselves and us." But those who "become completely Americanized . . . stand on exactly the same plane as descendants of any Puritan, Cavalier, or Knickerbocker among us, and do their full and honorable share of the nation's work."[16] They stand, Roosevelt (descendant of a Knickerbocker) was saying, on exactly the same plane as himself.

One reason for WASP complacency is surely that none of the non-WASP others separately, nor all of them together, offered any coherent or attractive alternative way of life. Where there is no threat, there should be no anxiety. Foreign things—bagels, banjos, burritos, beer steins—posed no threat at all. You can change a menu without changing your taste, and for most of American history that is what WASPs did, with strange words, skills, objects, edibles. New things, after all, might be useful, in which case it would be wrong not to use them. Many new things burrowed into American life so securely that they were absorbed and reexported, with the label "MADE IN THE USA." Thus, on the outskirts of Panama City one finds a Taco Bell.

Cultural contributions that were more than random items were more problematic. An activity or a belief that implies or proclaims a different view of the world is less easy to make use of than pizza or Santa Claus. Yet even here WASPs exercised considerable adaptive powers. If a potentially alien force could be seen as unserious, and therefore beneath notice, it could be allowed to fill a gap in the national pattern without disturbing the pattern. It ran free in WASP backyards as fun (the fate of jazz). Counter-philosophies that were unmistakably earnest were made to conform in their externals. Their domestic affairs, so to speak, may have remained unchanged, but their foreign policy was transformed (the fate of the Catholic Church). Ideas that did not slip into the mainstream bobbed in it, insoluble and unabsorbed. Socialism offers a case in point. There is an indigenous WASP radicalism, of the Populists and *Looking Backward;* a little earlier, of abolition and women's suffrage. European socialism, as practiced by Jews in New York and Germans in Milwaukee, was a political curiosity, less significant than Prohibition. The modern Socialist party used as its front man Norman Thomas, a former Presbyterian minister.

The fact is, there was no challenge that non-WASPs were capable of mounting that could have undermined the cultural hegemony of a group as large, as central, and as entrenched as the WASPs in America. The great majority of others, preoccupied with becoming a part of the WASP world themselves, offered no such challenge.

But, of course, challenges do not come only from outside.

5

★

WASPs, and Other Worlds They Aspired To

*H*OW HARD IS IT to be a WASP? The way of the WASP, after all, makes demands of WASPs themselves, as well as other people. It isn't only laborers from Canton or Calabria who have to adjust to its requirements.

For millions of WASPs, obviously, the adjustment was not hard at all. For millions more, life in a WASP world entailed every imaginable degree of difficulty, from annoyance to lunacy and suicide, though they never associated their problems with WASPhood. Some few in every generation, sensing incompatibility, pack up and leave; we shall mention the artistic exiles in a later chapter. And some, finding the rules not to their liking, rewrite them, either as individuals—Henry Adams, Ralph Waldo Emerson, Woodrow Wilson—or in groups. Singly or together, they become internal exiles, dreaming of new worlds even as outsiders aspire to join theirs.

The family background of Henry Adams makes George Bush's look *nouveau*. He was, of course, the great-grandson of the second president and the grandson of the sixth—a childhood familiarity with eminence charmingly described in his autobiography. "It was unusual for boys"—he and his brother are in church in Quincy, Massachusetts—"to sit behind a President grandfather, to read over his head, the tablet in memory of a President great-grandfather, who had 'pledged his life, his fortune, and his sacred honor' to serve the independence of his country and so forth, but boys

naturally supposed, without much reasoning, that other boys had
the equivalent of President grandfathers. . . . The Irish gardener
once said to the child: 'You'll be thinkin' you'll be President too!'
The casualty of the remark made so strong an impression on his
mind that he never forgot it. He could not remember ever to have
thought on the subject; to him, that there should be a doubt of his
being President was to him a new idea." A few years later he was
taken to the White House to visit Zachary Taylor, the twelfth
president. "Outside, in a paddock in front, 'Old Whitey,' the President's charger, was grazing, as they entered; and inside, the President was receiving callers as simply as if he were in the paddock
too."[1] After John Quincy, the Adams family's political fortunes
declined rather sharply; the closest Henry's father, Charles Francis,
ever got to the White House was third parties—a vice presidential
nomination on the Free Soil ticket of 1848, rejection by the Liberal
Republican convention of 1872—which weren't very close. He did
serve, however, in the House and the Senate and, during the Civil
War, as American Ambassador in London, where he labored to
prevent England from actively backing the Confederacy. Henry
was his private secretary during those years, after which he went on
to teach and write history, to edit the *North American Review,* to
travel, and to study a variety of subjects from geology to the Middle
Ages.

You have a hard time learning any of this from *The Education of
Henry Adams,* privately printed in his sixties and not published until
1918, the year of his death. One barrier is the style, which is
controlled by the use of an unrelentingly arch third person. Some
readers love it, others detest it. Herbert Hoover called *The Education*
"the puerilities of a parasite."[2] Adams's style yields all manner of
good things, except relief. "The mania for handling all sides of
every question, looking into every window, and opening every
door, was, as Bluebeard judiciously pointed out to his wives, fatal to
their practical usefulness in society."[3] Reading one page of this is
bracing; reading five hundred is like eating a bag of meringues.

The greater barrier to understanding is Adam's world view. *The
Education* offers itself as a record of what ideas and experiences
"turned out to be useful, and what not." The structural irony of the
book, of which Adams makes much—too much—is that most of
what he learned and did had no use at all. He finds years later that
his understanding of English diplomacy during the Civil War was

wrongheaded. He goes into journalism because "any man who was fit for nothing else could write an editorial." He studies fossils to learn about evolution, and concludes there is nothing to it but purposeless change. He introduces seminar teaching on the German model to Harvard, though he knows "from his own experience that his wonderful method led nowhere."[4] After many political defeats and disappointments, he takes up residence on Lafayette Square, as the best vantage for observing the house across the way, which he had first visited as a boy. Adams offers *The Education* as an extension of Franklin's *Autobiography*. It is more like a skit on it.

Adams explains his political apartness on ideological grounds: His family, even in the days of its presidents, was opposed to the business interests of Boston; once the whole country became a "bankers' Olympus," a faithful Adams must be even more isolated. We know from outside testimony that Adams was not as aloof as he professed to be. Adams and his wife, noted Henry James, "are eagerly anxious to hear what I have seen and heard at places which they decline to frequent. . . . After I had dined with Blaine, to meet the president, they fairly hung upon my lips."[5] But we don't need outsiders to tell us. *The Education* offers testimony to Adams's enduring interest in politics. Adams traveled with congenial senators; his best friend was McKinley's and Roosevelt's secretary of state. What is more, he understood politics: Some of his thoughts on Russia, years before the revolution, are still pertinent. Yet he must always seem to know and want to know less than he does. He adopts the mandarin manner and affects it when he does not feel it.

Adams abandoned two WASP character traits. The most obvious was the principle of use. So little in his life, he was pleased to say, had been useful. Some WASPs ponder their purposes; most take them as givens. Adams pondered and found none. Since nothing in his life turned out to be useful, he could reconcile himself to his lack of success (what use would it have been?). He could also throw dust into the eyes of his readers about his considerable, and disdained, industry.

His second abandonment concerned the guiding role of conscience, a force he replaced with amusement. The word runs through the book like a chime. "He cared not," he records himself thinking in 1893 of his education, "whether it were worth finishing, if only it amused."[6] It is a detached and rather affectless amusement, akin to depression. Still, it was the force which guided him. The great-grandson of the man who pledged life, fortune, and sacred honor for independence "and so forth," pledged his own for his exceedingly juiceless conception of a good time.

The other place in Massachusetts, besides bankers' Boston, where Adams felt ill at ease was philosophic Concord. "To the Concord Church," wrote Henry, "all Adamses were minds of dust and emptiness . . . politicians of doubtful honesty; natures of narrow scope."[7] The Adamses reciprocated the dislike, with some reason. In Concord of the 1840s and 1850s were to be found the peaks not only of American literature but of American lunacy as well. There were other hotbeds. Upstate New York during the same decades was a veritable California, teeming with Shakers, Mormons, table-rappers, and expecters of the millennium. A cult of perfectionists in Oneida practiced sexual communism with (the WASP touch) no ejaculation. In New York City Horace Greeley, the man who later beat Charles Francis Adams out of the Liberal Republican presidential nomination, advocated phrenological tests for train conductors. Orson and Lorenzo Fowler, the brothers who popularized phrenology, also pushed the virtues of octagonal houses, a campaign that collapsed when the cesspool of one of their buildings infected the well water, and the inhabitants came down with typhoid.

Yet Adams disdained the great along with the trivial. He dismissed Ralph Waldo Emerson's critique of Christianity as "naif." Here was a true failure of education.

Emerson's publishing career spanned forty years. His most interesting works, for our purposes, are his earliest, which also happen to be his best, from *Nature* (1836) to his second book of *Essays* (1844).

Any consideration of Emerson must begin with his style. Style may seem like an externality, a secondary factor. Yet anyone who wishes to be read with attention must first be read.

There are days which occur in this climate, at almost any season of the year, wherein the world reaches its perfection; when the air, the heavenly bodies and the earth make a harmony, as if Nature would indulge her offspring; when, in these bleak upper sides of the planet, nothing is to desire that we have heard of the happiest latitudes, and we bask in the shining hours of Florida and Cuba; when everything that

WASPs, and Other Worlds They Aspired To

has life gives sign of satisfaction, and the cattle that lie on the ground seem to have great and tranquil thoughts. These halcyons may be looked for with a little more assurance in that pure October weather which we distinguish by the name of the Indian summer. The day, immeasurably long, sleeps over the broad hills and warm wide fields. To have lived through all its sunny hours, seems longevity enough.[8]

Emerson is artful. He brings in Florida and Cuba to give a sense of spaciousness, cattle to come back down to earth. The aphoristic shape of the last sentence comes just before we might feel out of breath. At the same time, he seems artless, because effortless. This is only half a paragraph. The other half flows in the same way, with the same serenity; and all the other paragraphs in the essay; and all the essays in the book. You may find prose that is more exciting, or more dense, but nothing that is more pure. Next to this, the most famous American stylists fall away, abashed. Thoreau and Hemingway seem fussy and mannered; Melville, grand but turgid; Faulkner, turgid.

As with Henry Adams, the style matches the mind. The mark alike of Emerson's prose and thought is confidence. He set the tone in the introduction to *Nature*. "Undoubtedly we have no questions to ask which are unanswerable."[9] It's hard to say which is more astonishing, the assertion itself, or the *undoubtedly*. What Emerson is so confident of is simply that, practically speaking, you are the only thing in the universe. "Practically speaking," because he acknowledges and from time to time discusses many other things as well—time, history, art, religion, other people. But he holds them of little account. You are the measure by which they are judged. You also partake of them, create them, surpass them, if you will. You are God.

If we don't believe that this is what Emerson is saying, that is because we are not paying attention. Oddity may dazzle or habit deaden us. But this is the plain sense of his words. "Let us stun and astonish the intruding rabble of men and books and institutions by a simple declaration of the divine fact. Bid the invaders take the shoes from off their feet, for God is here within."[10]

Emerson believes in the unity of existence—that everything is one thing: everything is in you, and you are in everything. This could be understood to mean that we are all cells, cogs in Nature; it acts, we obey. But Emerson is not a man to lose sleep over causality.

If Nature is truly in you, it doesn't much matter which of you acts. And since the point of vantage from which everything is seen—the transparent eyeball—is yours, it is simplest to say that you are the center of everything.

Resting at the hub, what an enormous number of things a man is able to do without. Reading Emerson is like watching some stupefying auction. Is *that* going? and that? and that too?

History gets knocked down for a song. "Why all this deference to Alfred and Scanderbeg and Gustavus? Suppose they were virtuous; did they wear out virtue?" So does art. "The Greek sculpture is all melted away, as if it had been statues of ice; here and there a solitary figure or fragment remaining, as we see flecks and scraps of snow left in cold dells and mountain clefts in June and July. For the genius that created it creates now somewhat else."[11] This will not shock, for the WASP, as we have noted, never had much use for history or art.

But all forms of social activity are sold as cheap. "Nature will not have us fret and fume. . . . When we come out of the caucus, or the bank, or the Abolition-convention, or the Temperance-meeting, or the Transcendental-club into the fields and woods, she says to us, 'So hot? my little Sir.' "[12] So much for success, and civic-mindedness.

The main thrust of Emerson's attack, however, is against Christianity, the keeper of WASP conscience. "As men's prayers are a disease of the will, so are their creeds a disease of the intellect." Emerson's father had been pastor of Boston's First Church, and for three years, as a young man, Emerson was pastor in Boston's Second Church, until he found its doctrines too burdensome. Since these were the doctrines of Unitarianism, he perhaps didn't have much to shuck, though his 1838 address to the graduating class of Harvard Divinity School managed to raise even Unitarian hackles. In deference to his training and his environment, he still makes admiring references to Jesus, but Emerson's Jesus is rather like Emerson. "He said . . . 'I am divine. Through me, God acts; through me, speaks. Would you see God, see me; or see thee, when thou also thinkest as I now think.' "[13] This is a more radical challenge to conscience than Adams's wry appeal to amusement. Seeing with inner light is very different from generating it.

Though perhaps the most remarkable thing about Emerson was how little ruckus he caused in the WASP world whose ways he so serenely flouted. Three decades after Harvard condemned him, he was serving as an overseer. It is true that in the second half of his life he lost his nerve; there are signs of retreat as early as the second series of essays. Being God, it seems, was no easier than being a WASP. The smoothness and mildness of his rhetoric may have concealed its import. His very quotability worked against him. Taken out of context, any third sentence in Emerson is apt to sound like useful and practical advice. Since WASPs love the useful, they took the advice and forgot the context. For a century and a half we have juggled what we thought were platitudes, not knowing they were dynamite.

Allan Bloom has argued that the woes of the modern American mind are due to a Germanic invasion: Nietzsche, Heidegger, and Freud sweeping over the defenseless prairies like Guderians of the intellect. Adams and Emerson suggest that WASPs did not have to wait for invaders, but could nourish insurrections at home—and in prominent places. WASP America's most popular and most eloquent philosopher, and the scion of one of its oldest political dynasties, were no common defectors from the WASP's world.

In 1912, a defector made it to the White House.

Although Woodrow Wilson was a two-term president, he was nowhere near as popular as Theodore Roosevelt or Grant had been. He won his first election only because of a split in the Republican party—two Republicans, William Howard Taft and Roosevelt, were seeking the office at the same time. Four years later the Republicans had reunited, and their candidate, Charles Evans Hughes, went to bed on election night expecting to wake as president-elect. But Wilson narrowly carried California because of local Republican feuding there, and so squeezed to a second victory. By the end of his second term, public opinion on his record was unambivalent. Wilson was a broken man who had broken his party.

Yet his influence on political thought—on the thought of the politically thoughtful—was greater than any other politician's of this century, including FDR. Wilson's dreams of a new post-WASP world had far more direct impact than Adams or Emerson's, for he changed the terms of domestic American politics. He did it by offering a new way to think about conscience.

Wilson, wrote Digby Baltzell, "symbolized, the passing of the intellectual and spiritual leadership in America from the church to the university, from the preacher in the pulpit to the professor in the classroom."[14] Wilson's first scholarly article, on the American cabinet, had been published while he was at Princeton, where he, like many Southerners, had gone to college. In his thirties he returned to his alma mater to teach political science.

Wilson's specialty was American government, especially its defects, which had manifested themselves in "a marked and alarming decline in statesmanship" after the Civil War. The cause was to be found in the Constitution itself, in "the piecing of authority, the cutting of it up into small bits, which is contrived in our constitutional system." (Wilson's style, unlike Adams's or Emerson's, is not worth pondering. It was middling: worse than good, better than any living pol one can think of offhand.) Wilson early on became convinced that the British, with one source of political authority, a parliamentary majority, and one leader, the Prime Minister, did things better. For years he tinkered with schemes for adopting British elements here, and otherwise rendering the American system "strong, prompt, wieldy and efficient."[15]

His interest in these questions was not academic. Henry Adams had turned from politics to education. Wilson, the educator, burned to be in politics. In his late twenties he angled, unsuccessfully, for a job in the State Department. In his late forties, when he finally began to achieve his first positions of power, he put his theories of statesmanship into practice. In 1902 he became president of Princeton and behaved, in the words of biographer Arthur Link, like "Princeton's prime minister." When his plans to abolish the school's eating clubs ran into resistance, he made a cross-country tour of alumni associations—an "appeal to his constituents"[16]—to drum up support. He lost. He was saved from later imbroglios by an offer from New Jersey Democrats to run for governor in 1910. Wilson, though by then known as a progressive, was the candidate of the Hudson County machine, then as now the most corrupt in state politics. When a progressive Republican pointed this out during the campaign, Wilson loftily stiffed his own supporters, on prime ministerial grounds. "If I am elected, I shall understand that I am chosen leader of my party and the direct representative of the whole people."[17] This time he won.

But Wilson's concerns were not simply structural or personal. He had definite ideas about the kind of leadership that ought to be provided (ideally, by himself). As governor and president Wilson pushed a number of reforms—utilities commissions, the income tax, low tariffs. What was more interesting about him, and what marked him as a defector from the way of the WASP, was his intellectual style, what he saw as problems, and how he approached them. In *Constitutional Government*, Wilson's last book before graduating from political science to politics, he compared the well-led nation to a boat. "We say of a boat skimming the water with light foot, 'How free she runs,' when we mean how perfectly she is adjusted to the force of the wind. . . . Throw her head up into the wind and see how she will halt and stagger. . . . She is free only when you have let her fall off again and get once more her nice adjustment to the forces she must obey and cannot defy."[18] What sort of "adjustments" did Wilson have in mind? Eighteen years before *Constitutional Government*, in a speech called "Leaders of Men," he had used another boat metaphor, which was more explicit. "The captain of a Mississippi steamboat had made fast to the shore because of a thick fog lying upon the river. . . . An impatient passenger inquired the cause of the delay. 'We can't see to steer,' said the captain. 'But all is clear overhead,' suggested the passenger, 'you can see the North Star.' 'Yes,' replied the officer, 'but we are not going that way.'" By the North Star, where the boat wasn't going, Wilson meant a certain unusable kind of principle: "rounded, perfect, ideal." Principles "as statesmen conceive them" are something else again: "threads to the labyrinth of circumstances." The ship of state, Wilson concluded, back in the river, must follow the channel of circumstances in which it finds itself. If "it steer by the stars it will run aground."[19]

Wilson performs variations on the theme of adjustment and circumstance throughout *Constitutional Government*. "[P]olitical liberty is the right of those who are governed to adjust government to their own needs and interests. . . . Liberty fixed in unalterable law would be no liberty at all . . . the Constitution of the United States is not a mere lawyers' document: it is a vehicle of life, and its spirit is always the spirit of the age."[20] And what supplies the circumstances? Not the laws of history. Wilson claimed to have no magic dialectical key. But surely history itself, as we experience it, and as it brings new "needs and interests" to the fore. In a word, progress. For many historians, the political scientist Charles Kesler observes of all this, there are two Wilsons, "the conservative southern Democrat and dyed-in-the-wool Burkean and, after about 1910 [two years after *Constitutional Government*], the more familiar progressive reformer and idealistic crusader."[21] They shouldn't puzzle. There was only one of him. History is the link. Burke flipped forward into the future is progress.

To understand Wilson is to understand the word "progressive," which dominated the politics of the first decade and a half of this century. Most national leaders and would-be leaders wanted to be progressives. Roosevelt created a third party bearing the name. William Jennings Bryan was considered to be an ally, salt-of-the-earth division, until he got bogged down in Genesis. Even the Democrat Wilson beat to win his first nomination, the otherwise unremembered Champ Clark, claimed the label. Wilson superseded them all, at least briefly. More important, he possessed a superior theoretical self-consciousness. He knew best what he was about.

Progressivism represented a revolution in politics not because it changed people's goals—not because it brought in utility commissions or the Federal Reserve—but because it changed their notions of what a goal was. Progress was not progress toward anything definite ("we're not going that way"). It was going with the flow, waiting in the baggage claim area of history to see what rumbled up the belt next.

This is what marks Wilson, no less than Adams or Emerson, as a rebel. WASPs do think of principles as being like stars, as being "rounded, perfect, ideal." If they weren't, why bother with them? Wilson thus had a distorting effect on WASP notions of conscience as well as on their political practice. Adams shrugged off conscience in order to amuse himself, Emerson inflated it into "God . . . here within." Wilson tuned it to the "spirit of the age."

The progressive project and Wilson's advocacy of it were laden with ironies. Wilson was a lifelong Anglo-American democrat, and democracy was what he confidently expected to see coming out of history's hold—not in 1989, but in 1919. The next few years instead brought bolshevism, fascism, and national socialism. Wilson lived to see the first of these, and it was a rude shock to him. Detachments of Americans troops went to Russia during the Bolshevik Revolution to fight the wrong kind of progress. So progressives seem disingenuous, when they pass their preferences off as history, and flatfooted when rivals appear claiming a different historical dispensation.

Progressivism was also supposed to be a unifying ideology, drawing the nation together into a community. If the state is a boat, everyone was supposed to be in the same one. In later years, after Wilson's death, it became apparent that the political effect of progressivism was instead fragmenting. Since the next wave of history might come from anywhere, anyone was in practice entitled to claim that he was riding it. All these claims must be accommodated. Progressive politicians still talk from time to time about the nation as a community—a recent instance was Mario Cuomo's trope about the family of America—but they build their support in coalitions. It is hard to pitch one WASP character trait overboard without affecting all the others; in progressive politics, civic-mindedness sank soon after conscience.

The great personal irony of Wilson's career was that he was the opposite of a shrewdly adjusting progressive pilot. There were times when he maneuvered successfully and skillfully, but given a setback, he froze like a deer in headlights. "Men of ordinary physique and discretion cannot be Presidents and live,"[22] he had written in 1908, it turned out prophetically. His stubbornness ruined his politics and his health.

It didn't diminish his influence. Wilson gave both Franklin Roosevelt and Herbert Hoover their first posts at the national level. Late in his life Hoover honored Wilson with an admiring biography. Wendell Willkie began as a Wilson Democrat; Wilson's example inspired Dean Acheson to become one. Richard Nixon admired Wilson more than any other president. Not all of these men were clear, of course, about the extent of their hero's deviations from the way of the WASP; Hoover, amazingly, called Wilson a Jeffersonian. It didn't matter whether they were clear or not, only whether they and other politicians followed his example, and that mattered a great deal. For the first time, a new world had been imagined, not at a lectern or in a memoir, but on Pennsylvania Avenue.

There is one other way for the dissatisfied to defect from the WASP world: in a group. The group, in turn, catalyzes or creates wider dissatisfaction, drawing more defectors.

The WASP world has spun off numerous groups of self-made others, like rogue satellites; in the eighteenth and nineteenth centuries they generally took the form of new religions. For many years Unitarianism was the most important. It may be unfair to call Unitarianism an entirely new religion, but it pushed the boundaries of Protestantism pretty hard. The church in which the Adamses worshiped, described by Henry, was Unitarian. So is the most unusual church in New England, King's Chapel in Boston, which defected not from Congregationalism (the usual route) but from Anglicanism. The one time I looked into it, an aged, crisp-spoken woman, sitting on a stool to answer the questions of tourists, explained its practices thus: "We still say the *chaunts,* though we don't believe in the Holy Ghost." The new religions that endured had a way of settling down, sinking into stable cultural orbits: The Christian Scientists publish a newspaper; the Mormons run Utah. Others—the Jehovah's Witnesses—have remained hostile and separate, as distinct from the mainstream of WASP life as Hutterites.

Whatever the religion, the psychology of conversion is always the same. The convert believes that the life he once led was blamable, and that he was, in some degree, to blame for it. He believed in falsehoods, therefore he lived falsely. Exchanging false beliefs for true ones involves changing himself. This sense of personal responsibility for past errors may be what kept many of the post-WASP religions culturally so docile.

This century, however, has seen a proliferation of defecting groups with a different attitude.

In 1930 twelve Southerners took a look at their region and its prospects. Several of them—Allen Tate, Robert Penn Warren— were, or would become, individually famous. But their credo, *I'll Take My Stand,* with its title boldly taken from "Dixie," was a call for cultural secession. They argued that the South was, and had always been, a feudal rural society whose only hope lay in casting off industrialism, the economic form the WASP world had taken. The most consistent contributors wanted the South to spurn Jefferson and Protestantism as well.[23]

Nothing much came of Agrarianism, but the manifesto exemplified a new mood for self-made others. Unlike Mormons, new defectors underwent no transforming conversion. The only change they felt obliged to make was in their attitude toward the WASP world, which they now judged to be inferior. *They* had been all right all along. Their woes came from the WASP world's oppression of them. It might have to change; they didn't. This is the reverse of the process undergone by immigrants. It is a process of de-assimilation.

Later groups of self-made others had more impact. Many of them took as their model the most conspicuous case of separateness in sight, blacks. We have already looked, in chapter one, at Norman Mailer's reveries about the liberating influence of black low life. The beats felt the same impulse. "At lilac evening I walked with every muscle aching among the lights of 27th and Welton in the Denver colored section, wishing I were a Negro."[24] (As if blacks didn't have enough to put up with, without having to bear the projections of frisky whites). In the sixties a whole class of self-made others came into being—young people. "We used to think of ourselves as little clumps of weirdos," Janis Joplin announced from the stage at Woodstock. "But now we're a whole new minority group."[25] The student radical avant-garde was at first a Jewish movement, with a sprinkling of upper-class Protestants. But lower-class Christian kids soon joined in, with the result that it became much more violent (*goyishe kops*).[26] Beyond this tiny political core were the large numbers of essentially normal kids who just wanted to feel sad, get high, and get laid.

As their decade progressed, another class of self-created others announced itself: women. Relatively speaking, in a world full of clitorectomy and polygamy—where Chinese baby girls are regularly murdered by their disappointed parents and Hindu widows are still occasionally burned on the pyres of their husbands—female WASPs were blessed among women. In another era they won passage of the 18th Amendment, soon followed by the 19th Amendment for themselves. The first women's suffrage in the world had been in the Territory of Wyoming. But risen expectations called forth another revolution, with blacks again serving as a model of oppressed otherness. The Equal Rights Amendment sought to mimic the Civil Rights Acts. A second sexual revolution, of preference not gender, was declared by homosexuals in the 1970s.

De-assimilation became the norm for entire groups of non-WASPs. Instead of pondering how to fit in, they sought ways of striking out on their own. Hispanics proclaimed what amounted to a right to resist learning English. Michael Dukakis, playing to such pressures, spoke several sentences of his convention acceptance speech in Spanish. Black separatism, spreading beyond fringe groups like the Black Panthers or the pseudo Islam of Louis Farrakhan, inflected even the rhetoric of a mainstream black politician like Jesse Jackson, who could speak warmly of the Statue of Liberty in one breath, of Third World tyrants in the next. "I'm a Third World person," he once told an interviewer, "I grew up in an occupied zone"[27] (he had grown up in Greenville, South Carolina). What was notable about these manifestations was not that they occurred—the ethnic history of America is full of particularist tugs—but that they were approved and often encouraged by the general culture.

Defections from the general culture were occurring at a great rate. In each case the cause of flight, the bad past the defectors wanted to leave behind, as desperately as immigrants wanted to leave Odessa or Cork, was the world of the WASP. The enemy of every wayward impulse—of black pride, mother tongues, pot, frisbees, matriarchy, fisting, the Southern way of life, whatever—was conscience, industry, success, and all the rest: the way of the WASP.

But this is running ahead. Before we can diagnose, or even discuss, such developments, we need a better look at what exactly happened, and why. It is possible that this rash of defection and discontent emerged because the world of the WASP finally became unendurable. The beast of the soul, loaded and overloaded, fell to its knees and moved no more. That is a conceivable explanation. It is certainly the explanation that the self-made others would give. The convergence of so much, in a matter of years, suggests another possibility: that the WASP character itself had changed, allowing, even encouraging rebellions against itself. America had taken a detour from the way.

We have said that non-WASPs could not have brought about such a change on their own. Henry Adams and Ralph Waldo Emerson show how the desire for detours could arise spontaneously among WASPs themselves. Woodrow Wilson represented a detour that political and moral discourse actually took. In the next three chapters we shall look at WASP ways and their interaction with three areas of American life: Wall Street, the arts, and the Protestant churches (their churches). We shall see, in each area, varieties of failure or revolt, touching, in succession, on every important character trait: industry, success, and civic-mindedness; use and anti-sensuality; last, and most importantly, conscience. We shall discover a class of defectors as influential as the political progressives. We will then be in a position to speculate, finally, why the world of the WASP slipped its orbit, and how it might be brought back.

6

✦

Wall Street,
At Home and Abroad

WHEN MIKHAIL GORBACHEV, then riding high, visited New York City on one of his barnstorming tours of the West, he passed briefly but deliberately over the street that has given its name to the economic system he seemed eager to learn from even though he was committed, *ex officio*, to superseding it.

Gorbachev was scheduled to visit the World Trade Center towers, and for a while it was rumored that he might go the few blocks east and actually visit the floor of the Stock Exchange. That turned out to be unworkable, so he arranged the next best thing, a drive-by.

The route ran past the Exchange up Broad Street, then left two quick blocks on Wall Street before turning uptown to the next engagement. The Stock Exchange Christmas tree, tall and shaggy, was already standing in the middle of Broad Street, giving Gorbachev two alien symbols to contend with instead of one. A largish crowd of the curious gathered beneath the looming temples of Mammon to see him pass. There wasn't much to see—a rush of motorcycle cops, police cars with cherries flashing, and black limos with curiously Victorian side curtains, making it impossible to tell which car contained the postulant. In a blur, they were gone. PR, as in perestroika.

When we think of Wall Street today, we think, as Gorbachev thought, of money. It is an obvious thing to think of. Since New York replaced Philadelphia as the nation's banking center, Wall Street has been the place where people who have money and people who need it are matched, in the hope that more money will ensue—ideally, for those who supply it and those who make use of it, as well as for the matchmakers. If the business of America is capitalism, the business of Wall Street is generating the capital.

There was a time, however, when thinking of Wall Street also meant thinking of government—and not just in the sense, beloved of conspiracy theorists and socialists, that plutocrats told politicians what to do. For a half-century, from the 1900s to the 1950s, men associated with Wall Street, mostly but not entirely corporate lawyers, became politicians and public servants. They interested themselves in national affairs at home and abroad. Such interest was assumed as a reality, however much it was resented. When the *Chicago Tribune* wrote of Thomas Dewey, former district attorney, former corporate lawyer, and governor of New York, that he had gone "to Downing Street by way of Wall Street,"[1] it was speaking in isolationist shorthand, but it was not speaking of nothing. Wall Street's view of the world stressed the importance of American engagement in foreign affairs, particularly those of Europe, and most particularly (the *Tribune* was fulminating in 1943) those of England. Logically, it is perilous to erect a symbol—Wall Street—for a collectivity, and then hold up an individual—Dewey—as an epitome of the symbol. But if the individuals are prominent enough, as many internationally minded Wall Streeters after Dewey would be, and many before him had been, the compression makes sense.

Wall Street's former sense of civic responsibility offered one answer to the child's-eye question that confronts every businessman, whether he knows it or not: Why spend ten hours a day in an office? "That every American should make money," wrote Logan Pearsall Smith, a renegade Philadelphia gentleman of the turn of the century, "that even those who already possessed it should devote their lives to making more, that all of them without exception should betake themselves every morning to their offices and spend all the hours of sunlight in these great business buildings—this was the universally accepted and grotesque ideal of life in the world we live in."[2] How does one answer the Smiths of the world? Economists can explain the behavior of businessmen, but their explanations are singularly unsatisfying. Followers of Marx would say that private vice serves the good of a class. Followers of the other Smith, Adam, would say that private vice serves the good of all, which is scarcely more inspiring. The public servants of Wall Street provided more compelling justification for sitting in an office ten hours a day: If you did it honorably and effectively, you might be called upon to sit in the offices of the government and serve the nation directly.

These politicians of Wall Street were WASPs, by birth or training. Oscar Straus, the first Jewish Cabinet member, came out of the parallel universe of German-Jewish finance, which resembled Protestant Wall Street in every cultural particular. James Forrestal may have been the son of Irish Catholic immigrants, but before he became president of Dillon, Read and the first secretary of defense he had been a member of Princeton's Cottage Club. Wall Street's public servants were a random lot socially in the beginning, unremarkable in their background or training, though as their day in the sun drew to a close, they tended to come from a particular mold. Then the mold changed. Wall Street stayed home, as others took up the civic burden.

But first the money. Wall Street was generating a lot of it in the 1980s. The October 1987 crash seemed to be only a hiccup; it didn't deflect Gorbachev. Indeed, there was a widespread feeling that there was too much money about, a generalized discomfort at the sight of people getting rich, and a sharp suspicion that some of the riches were ill-gotten.

In May 1986 the SEC charged Dennis Levine, a mergers and acquisitions specialist at Drexel Burnham Lambert, with insider trading. Levine, pleading guilty, agreed to work with the prosecutors, setting off a firecracker string of indictments and convictions. Levine fingered arbitrageur Ivan Boesky, who agreed to help the government in its pursuit of Drexel Burnham and its (to enemies) junk-bond or (to friends) high-yield-bond wizard Michael Milken. Drexel settled with the government early in 1989, leaving Milken to fend for himself. A year later, Drexel was bankrupt, and Milken had copped a plea. The unfolding tale was spiced with juicy tidbits: Bahamanian banks and tips passed on pay phones, life styles of the rich and infamous. It was not as lurid as Richard Whitney, the president of the Stock Exchange who went to jail in 1938 for misappropriation of funds (the headmaster of Groton visited his old boy in Sing Sing), but it was the next best thing. Good enough to float one of Wall Street's scourges, former U.S. attorney Rudolph Giuliani, into New York politics. Oliver Stone's *Wall Street,* shot as the first arrests were occurring, opened just weeks after the October crash to round-the-block lines. The crash itself seemed, in its first headlong days, to be God's judgment on greed. When the market picked itself up, the censorious went back to waiting grimly for the day of reckoning.

Sniffing around the Wall Street cases, more than one nose picked up an odor less savory than righteous zeal. "There is a lot of anti-Semitism at work," a Drexel employee told the journalist Connie Bruck. "People see Drexel as a bunch of Jewish guys who have been making too much money."[3] "The anti-Jewish arbitrageur jokes are all around the street," wrote A. M. Rosenthal two months after Boesky pleaded guilty to assorted sins. "Top Jewish figures in the industry," Rosenthal said, were meeting to prepare for a possible backlash.[4] "When the scandal on Boesky first came out," one invest-ment manager told me, "a number of my Jewish partners worried because all the people in the business were Jewish. They're still worried. But then," he added consolingly, if deflatingly, "they're always worried."

Certainly many of the players in the new money world of the eighties were Jews—more than enough to attract the attention of anti-Semites (one is more than enough). But not all were. Carl Lindner, a Cincinnati ice cream maker turned supermarket owner, and one of Milken's clients, was a Baptist. Another client of Milken was the Australian press magnate Rupert Murdoch. The common trait of the nouveaux was not Jewishness but newness. They were outsiders who came from strange places and behaved in strange ways. The annual Drexel Burnham High Yield Bond Conference, aka the Predators' Ball, half pep rally, half revival meeting, was no establishmentarian get-together when Michael Milken ran it. It was held not on the East Coast but in a Hilton hotel in Beverly Hills. Meetings began at 6:00 A.M., in deference to Michael Milken, who rose at 4:30. Milken had been born in the Valley, as in Valley Girls, and lived there still. At one conference investors were entertained by a video of Madonna, slinking and singing, "I'm a Double B girl in a high yield world, Drexel, Drexel, Drexel."

The culture of Wall Street had been changing for years. The arbitrageurs, the mergers and acquisitions specialists, and the bond impresarios were only the gaudy culmination. The change began with the influx of institution and pension fund investors in the sixties and seventies. These dealers in other people's money were not interested in long-term relations with brokers and bankers, the kind of partnership whose consummation occurred, as John Thomas of Lehman Brothers used to say, "not when they ask you how to price your bonds, but when they ask what college their kids should go to." The new investors wanted maximum immediate return on money. Wall Street met the new demands with new men, "rug merchant types, thinking in terms of 64ths, straddles and puts, not button-down types of days gone by who were in the firm because they'd grown up in it. Trading culture came into a white shoe world."[5]

Cultural clashes helped tear apart Lehman Brothers Kuhn Loeb, Wall Street's oldest investment banking partnership—at least, according to Lehman's premier obituarist, Ken Auletta. The main cause of Lehman's collapse and ingestion by Shearson/ American Express in 1984 had been the presence of two big fish, Peter Peterson and Lewis Glucksman, in a not big enough pond. The fatal feud between the two men was exacerbated, however, by the fact that Glucksman, an archetypal "rug merchant type," felt bottomless resentment over all the real and imagined snubs he had experienced in his climb to the top. "The son of middle class Hungarian Jews, he constantly inveighed against the 'Our Crowd' Jews in banking"—German, or first-wave, Jews. "Vividly, he remembers how one senior partner [at Lehman], decades earlier, advised him not to apply to join the Century Club in Westchester, an 'Our Crowd' bastion." Since the Century Club has had second-wave Jewish members since the 1920s, this bit of snobbery may well have had as much to do with personal characteristics as intra-Jewish pecking orders. What Glucksman resented were the manners of assimilation. What the old Jewish guard resented in him was his lack of any manners at all. For whatever reason, Glucksman felt put upon, and he focused his resentments on Peterson. The irony is that Peterson, né Petropoulos, son of a diner owner in Kearney, Nebraska, had risen from a lower class than Glucksman. But he had worked in a wider world—Assistant to the President for International Economic Affairs and Secretary of Commerce under Nixon, a wheel in the Council on Foreign Relations thereafter—and he let everyone know it. "On [Peterson's] office wall hung original paintings by Jasper Johns and Robert Motherwell, autographed pictures of former Soviet Premier Brezhnev, framed photographs of Peterson with former Presidents Nixon and Ford, with former Secretary of State Kissinger, with Nixon's entire Cabinet, with Japanese Prime Minister Nakasone."[6] Gee whiz. The larger irony, approaching pathos, is that anyone would feel belittled by such gross name-dropping and status display. But, as C. S. Lewis pointed out, the purpose of inner rings is to exclude. Anyone who feels excluded serves the purpose.

A second sin of Wall Street's new men, after rawness, was the open avowal they made of their own desires. "Greed," said Gordon Gekko, the antihero of *Wall Street,* echoing Ivan Boesky, "is good." Blasphemy. Greed cannot be good. Work is good; so is money. But they are good as signs, respectively, of devotion to industry and the achievement of success. No ripple of longing may pass between them. The new men were meddling with the mantra. No wonder they aroused anxiety and dislike.

A last trespass of theirs was to make plain a more general failing. By their bold pursuit of money, they forced Wall Street to acknowledge that its sense of political responsibility was a thing of the past. They made unashamedly manifest what was—guiltily?—latent. Ken Lipper, a partner at Lehman Brothers Kuhn Loeb and later a contributor to Oliver Stone's screenplay, remembers the old system, the system that produced Thomas Deweys, with nostalgia. "It was a Zen experience. You learned by example." Lipper joined the Council on Foreign Relations at age thirty; Cyrus Vance and George Ball—weighty examples—sponsored him for membership. "I raised my hand at my first meeting. Afterwards, a senior partner at Brown Brothers, Harriman said to me, 'Think if anyone else here wants to ask your question, or if anyone here knows the answer. If both answers are no, you might ask it. But you're better off waiting for a year before you say something.'"[7] This solemn initiation occurred in 1973, which was already very late in the day. Four years later Vance became Wall Street's last secretary of state. Three years after that, he resigned after losing a power struggle with the national security adviser, a Polish academic, by which time Michael Milken had held his second Predators' Ball. Is it fanciful to suggest that the new men, unconscious of any betrayal, acted as lightning rods for an older Wall Street's sense of faithlessness to its own lost ideals?

"The Department of State as it existed at the turn of the century, and as it still was in large measure in the 1920s when I entered it," wrote George Kennan, "was a quaint old place" with swinging doors, brass cuspidors, black leather rocking chairs, and in general a "law office atmosphere."[8] Well might it have had such an atmosphere, since so many of the people who ran it were Wall Street lawyers. The connection began in the 1900s, after America had begun acquiring its Caribbean and Pacific empire.

John Hay, the last secretary of state of the nineteenth century and the first of the twentieth, had nothing to do with Wall Street. His only connection to money was marrying it. His legal career began in Springfield, Illinois, where he studied in the office of Abraham Lincoln, whom he went on to serve as secretary in the White House. In 1874 he married the daughter of a Cleveland railroad magnate, whose fortune allowed him to write a Lincoln biography, a novel, and some comic poetry, to serve as a diplomat, and to maintain a friendship with Henry Adams.

Hay's successor at State, Elihu Root, had followed a different career path. Root had been active in New York law and politics since the 1860s. His first cabinet appointment came in 1899. "I was called to the telephone, and told by one speaking for President McKinley, 'The President directs me to say to you that he wishes you to take the position of Secretary of War.' I answered, 'Thank the President for me, but say that it is quite absurd, I know nothing about war, I know nothing about the army.' I was told to hold the wire, and in a moment there came back the reply, 'President McKinley directs me to say that he is not looking for anyone who knows anything about war or for anyone who knows anything about the army; he has got to have a lawyer to direct the government of these Spanish islands [the Philippines], and you are the lawyer he wants.'"[9] When Hay died in 1905, Root became secretary of state. The Nobel Peace Prize came his way in 1912, and he engaged in statesmanship and elder statesmanship for the next two decades. His career in domestic politics was less glittering; he served one term as a senator, when state legislatures still made the choice, and lost a half-hearted bid to win the Republican presidential nomination in 1916.

In the intervals of his public career, he continued his legal work. In the hiatus between his stints at War and State, Root was professionally involved in the squabble of two tycoons, E. H. Harriman and James J. Hill, over the pieces of a failed railroad trust scheme. The case is a nice example of a high-powered lawyer's life. "With Hill were lined up the Morgan interests, and with Harriman, those of Kuhn, Loeb and Company. It was characteristic of Root's practice that mere chance determined the side on which he was to take part." At noon one day, a representative of the Morgan-Hill group appeared in his office to ask him to defend their plan to liquidate the trust's stock. Root agreed. "About two o'clock on the same day,

Harriman called on him to ask him to accept a retainer to oppose this plan . . . Had Harriman arrived a little earlier, Root would have opposed before the courts the Hill-Morgan plan, instead of defending it."[10] Root's clients won.

The man who won the presidential nomination Root sought was another former New York lawyer, Charles Evans Hughes. Hughes, as we have seen, went on to lose the election, making the presidency about the only high office he never held. He had begun his law practice in the 1880s. In 1906 he was elected governor of New York, and Root gave a crucial speech on his behalf. President Taft appointed him to the Supreme Court, Harding and Coolidge chose him to be secretary of state, and Hoover brought him, at age sixty-eight, back to the Court as chief justice. In his career as a lawyer, Hughes had not been just the hired gun of giants like Hill and Harriman. He pursued the powers that be as well as defended them. His first fame came from investigations of corruption in the gas and insurance businesses (Root was a director of one of the insurance companies Hughes exposed). But he did his share of defending. In one famous case, after leaving the State Department, he successfully represented General Electric with the argument that the company had a vested interest in a radio frequency. That case inflamed populist sentiment when his nomination for chief justice came before the Senate.

Root's and Hughes's careers intersected at points, not always in a friendly fashion. Root's heir and protégé was Henry Stimson. Stimson began as a clerk in Root's law firm in 1891. Root got him his first public office, U.S. attorney for the southern district of New York, fifteen years later. "During my various excursions into public life," Stimson wrote at the end of his life, "I have always felt that I remained a lawyer with a law firm waiting as a home behind me."[11] His second excursion, an attempt to succeed Hughes as governor of New York, failed dismally; Taft appointed him to Root's old job, secretary of war, instead. Almost thirty years later Franklin Roosevelt, looking for bipartisan support for a policy of engagement in European affairs, made Stimson secretary of war again. (One of the speeches he made during his tenure, to the Andover graduating class of 1942, urged the young men to go to college before enlisting. George Bush ignored the advice.) In the interval Stimson had served as governor general of the Philippines and as Hoover's secretary of state. Stimson may have relied on the comforting image of his law firm, but he also believed that "the American lawyer should regard himself as a potential officer of his government . . . if the time should ever come when this tradition had faded out and the members of the bar had become merely the servants of business, the future of our liberties would be gloomy indeed."[12]

The backgrounds of these four secretaries of state mark an interesting social trajectory. None of the first three had come from the upper class. Hay was born in Salem, Indiana, the son of a typical small town post-frontier figure, a doctor/land speculator/owner and editor of newspapers. Root grew up in Clinton, New York, on the campus of Hamilton College, where his father taught geology and math. Hughes's father was an immigrant, a Welsh minister who came to America because he had been impressed by Franklin's *Autobiography.* The family lived here and there in upstate New York—Glens Falls, Oswego, Newark—and finally settled in Brooklyn. Stimson started on an altogether loftier plane. His father was an investment banker turned surgeon. Henry was sent to Andover, then Yale, where he made Skull and Bones, and Harvard Law School. None of the other men had gone to prep school; Hay never went to law school.

Hay, Root, and Hughes couldn't have gone to prep schools, as we understand them, because they hardly existed before the 1880s. Digby Baltzell lists the founding of Groton, in 1884, as one of the signs of the consolidation of a national upper class (the Social Register appeared three years later).[13] It was also a first whiff of Anglomania, the New England boarding school as surrogate for the playing fields of Eton.

We have come to the period of the Wise Men, the group of advisers to Roosevelt and Truman whose nickname was bestowed on them by McGeorge Bundy and popularized in a recent book of the same name. Several of them came straight from Wall Street. Averell Harriman (son of E. H.) founded his own investment banking firm, whose partners included Robert Lovett, another future Wise Man, and Prescott Bush. John McCloy, born to a poor Philadelphia family, became a Wall Street lawyer. Dean Acheson, interestingly, moved immediately after law school to Washington to practice international law, bypassing New York. Most of them belonged at birth to the new upper class, Harriman, born to the uppermost class, became a director of the Union Pacific railroad when he was a senior at Yale. During World War II he used the secret number of Skull and Bones for the combination lock of his diplomatic briefcase. Acheson, who was raised in much more modest circumstances, was nevertheless the son of an Episcopalian minister, later a bishop, who was a British subject to boot—all the social cachet a reasonable man could require. ("At the turn of the century," Baltzell notes, "and especially after the first World War . . . the Episcopal Church developed into a national upper class institution.")[14] Those that were not to the manner born passed through the necessary assimilating experiences, with more or less success. George Kennan, a tax lawyer's son from Milwaukee, went to Princeton because he had been seduced by *This Side of Paradise,* though he hated actually being there.

Republican internationalists and would-be leaders of the same period seem in retrospect like reversions to an earlier social type. Thomas Dewey, before he ran for governor of New York (successfully) and president (unsuccessfully), had been a New York lawyer and a nationally known prosecutor. Wendell Willkie, another failed Republican presidential candidate, was a former utilities executive. But they were both Midwesterners (from Owosso, Michigan, and Elwood, Indiana, respectively) who had gone to home state colleges. John Foster Dulles, the son of a Presbyterian minister from Watertown, New York, looks like even more of a throwback. But he was no ordinary minister's kid. His mother's father had been Benjamin Harrison's secretary of state, while her brother-in-law would be Woodrow Wilson's. Dulles's grandfather, John Foster, took him to the Second Hague Conference when he was nineteen. Dulles went to Princeton, the Sorbonne (a summer course with Henri Bergson), and Washington Law School, then slid into a Wall Street firm, where he waited for some Republican to win the presidency so that he might follow in his grandfather's and uncle's footsteps.

Dulles retained enough Presbyterianism to speak of the Cold War over which he presided in religious terms, which excited the contempt of the Wise Men and their fans. Yet his religious preoccupations were not unique. Acheson marked the unveiling of the Revised Standard Version of the Bible in a speech that, according to the *New York Times,* "portrayed the Bible . . . as having had a predominating role in shaping the national life of this country. . . . Secretary Acheson said that in the days of the early settlers 'the Book was all,' and that, in fact, the settlers 'came here to live their own reading of it.'"[15] (Nowadays the *Times* would run an op-ed piece gravely chiding him for such a sectarian outburst.) Charles

Evans Hughes lost the faith of his parents, at least in the form in which they practiced it. Prayers before meals, he wrote home early in his thirties, were "a wretched business. There is a life . . . so far above these petty observances."[16] Yet he taught Sunday school at the Fifth Avenue Baptist Church and served as president of the Northern Baptist Convention while he was governor of New York. When Elihu Root first moved to New York City in 1867, he gave lectures at the YMCA on such topics as "Mental Culture—a Christian Duty" and "Christianized Ambition" ("we rightly desire honor and distinction. . . . But [but!] always we must remember the glory is not ours").[17] Fifty years later he recommended YMCA stations to Dulles's uncle as a way of boosting morale in allied Russia.

The faith of the Wall Street politicians answers, even more convincingly than public service, the question, Why spend ten hours a day in an office? You spend time making money, and then serving the public, because conscience tells you it is right. Social Darwinism had a vogue in WASP churches toward the end of the nineteenth century. "No man in this land," preached Henry Ward Beecher, "suffers from poverty unless it be more than his fault—unless it be his sin."[18] But this is not what we're talking about. Social Darwinism was an extreme, and a hybrid—importing catch-phrases from politics and social science into Protestantism as liberation theology imports them into Catholicism today. WASP religion did not need such dubious assistance. Conscience had given its sanction to industry, success, and civic-mindedness before Darwin was born.

What happened to this breed of sometimes God-fearing, increasingly well-born, lawyerly, money-making men? The commonest explanation for their disappearance is that the Vietnam War, which the last generation of Wall Street public servants supported and then soured on, destroyed their self-confidence. Yet that cannot be the reason. Vietnam was as much the bright idea of academics and foreign policy experts, and they suffered no loss of confidence or authority as a class.

Dean Acheson's choice of law firm was a more significant straw in the wind. If one hankered after a career in Washington, it was increasingly unnecessary, even distracting, to incubate in New York. You simply set yourself up in D.C., in the permanent government in waiting.

Other career paths to power opened up. The man who recommended Dean Rusk to John Kennedy for secretary of state was Dean Acheson. Rusk had worked under Acheson during the Truman administration, and both men were sons of ministers, but that was about their only social or career resemblance. Rusk's father was a Presbyterian minister in poorest rural Georgia. After a Rhodes scholarship plucked him from poverty, Rusk became dean of a women's college; during the fifties he ran the Rockefeller Foundation. William Rogers and Cyrus Vance were both lawyers—Vance a Wall Street lawyer by way of the Kent School, Yale, and Yale Law— but their careers were frustrated and ultimately derailed by Henry Kissinger and Zbigniew Brzezinski, immigrant professors. When Kissinger was installed as secretary of state, succeeding Rogers, he made a poignant slip of the tongue. "There is no country in the world," he said, "where it is conceivable that a man of my origin could be standing here next to the President of the United States."[19] What he meant to say, of course, was that in no *other* country could such a prodigious thing have happened. Obviously it was conceivable in the United States; it was happening. In any case, he exaggerated; there is nothing prodigious, in this country, about a former refugee rising to the top if he has credentials in the right line of work, and by the sixties and seventies the knowledge industries had become a better line than bonds or antitrust. George Shultz, the longer serving of Ronald Reagan's secretaries of state, was another academic, author of such works as *Management Organization and the Computer* and "Wage Determination in the Men's Shoe Industry." Averell Harriman's partner's son picked a lawyer to replace Shultz. James Baker III even went to Princeton, but his LLB comes from the University of Texas at Austin, and his practice was all in the oil patch.

A process of double retreat set in. As Wall Street withdrew from political responsibility, government drew away from Wall Street. Industry was detached from civic-mindedness.

The institutional expression of Wall Street's half-century of intimacy with American foreign policy was the place where Ken Lipper was told not to speak for a year, the Council on Foreign Relations. I was a temporary member for five years (four of talking). I heard a Grenadian dictator there, and once sat next to Theodore Sorenson. The Council occupies a former mansion on Park Avenue, about the last on the street. Its discussions are civil and informed, its teacups are green and pink. If it weren't tied to the real estate, Irving Kristol has observed, it would be in Washington tomorrow. Even the conspiracy theorists, who for years spent so much energy cataloguing CFR memberships, have turned their attention to a hotter foreign policy talk shop, the Trilateral Commission, assembled in 1973 at David Rockefeller's behest by Zbigniew Brzezinski.

How well did the men from Wall Street do? "The mind of American statesmanship," wrote Kennan, "stemming as it does in so large a part from the legal profession in our country, gropes with unfailing persistence" for "formal criteria of a juridical nature" with which to tidy up the world and our relations to it.[20] McKinley, when an archipelago dropped into his lap, turned to a Wall Street lawyer to run it. The tincture of business legalism, or corporate lawyerliness, that suffused our foreign policy for the next fifty years helps explain both its self-interest and its idealism—two seemingly contrary impulses, puzzling perhaps to foreigners, but in fact related. A lawyer tries to get the best deal he can for his client, whence self-interest. But laws, by definition, imply a condition in which all clients, at least with respect to the laws, are equal, whence idealism.

Their idealism, on the other hand, stopped short of progressivism in foreign policy. If crusades for world peace or world democracy required treaties, Wall Street lawyers would happily draw them up. But crusading itself was not in their blood. Wendell Willkie's *One World,* an empty, effusive best-seller that would have embarrassed even Wilson—"Men and women all over the world are on the march," that kind of thing—was a sign of decay. "He has burst all the bonds," one reviewer noted, accurately and ominously, "of big-business thinking."[21] The open use of the formulas of realpolitik was a sign of decay in a different direction. It may be that American statesmen should act according to the rules of Metternich and Bismarck, as George Kennan and Henry Kissinger, in their very different ways, urged. Perhaps they always, unconsciously, had. But they had never said so.

All in all, they did an earnest job, though there was a falling off toward the end, personally as well as politically. Dulles's rigidity is widely disdained. Forrestal committed suicide. Harriman wasn't very bright. Acheson drank. They also had more difficult problems to deal with.

The increasing class-consciousness of the pool from which they were drawn was also a defect. This was a class wrinkle of the fifty-year phase of WASP clan-mindedness. The emphasis on the right prep schools, the right colleges, the right clubs at the right colleges (Lovett and Bundy, as well as Stimson and Harriman, were Skull and Bones; Acheson and Vance were Scroll and Key) smacks of aristocracy, and that smacks of trouble. How strong is a set of rules that needs such artificial buttressing, such elaborate inculcation? Hothouse virtues are not real virtues. The way that must be so carefully taught is not the way of the WASP.

Ask a bright young spark on Wall Street today why so few of his peers have any interest in Washington. You sit, perhaps, in a new office in Battery Park City with a view, half of other new offices in envelopes of taupe stone and green glass, half of New Jersey marshland. The Statue of Liberty stands toylike in a corner. Answers come readily. It's only good answers that are hard to come by.

Wall Street can still provide secretaries of the treasury—Donald Regan, Nicholas Brady. It can even supply a few diplomatic personnel, at below-top-drawer levels: Evan Galbraith, ambassador to France, and John Whitehead, deputy to George Shultz. In Whitehead's case, this was a capstone, a final move by a man who could go no farther and would stay no longer in the financial community. One reason for his unwillingness to stay on Wall Street was the advent of the rug merchants. "Part of the reason why I felt the time had come for me to step aside at Goldman Sachs [his pre-State job] was that the business had changed so much from what I was used to. . . . To have a company rely on your advice—to say, go ahead, do the issue now, or do a bond issue instead of a stock issue—well, that was a very responsible job. But when you're only asked to decide whether to bid 7.22 percent or 7.24 percent—that didn't quite seem important to me anymore."[22]

Such traffic as there now is between Wall Street and Washington mostly runs the other way, consisting of tired or out-of-office pols who want an infusion of cash. "The amount of money you can make in Wall Street," I was told in Battery Park City, "is a lot more than Forrestal ever made." Money is also the most commonly cited reason why Wall Street stays home. How can you reasonably expect a man to spend time in Washington, D.C., when there are such pots of gold to be found along Broad Street? "I don't think you see many people of my age group"—the speaker was a notch above my age group—"going from here to D.C. The pay cut is amazing."[23]

Another reason often cited is the present-day confirmation process. François de Saint Phalle, of Shearson Lehman Hutton, the monster firm that emerged from Peterson's and Glucksman's bickering, expounded this reservation with real passion. "Everything you've done in your life becomes open to investigation, to offensive, voracious attack and exposure. Did you ever cheat on a test? Nonsense like that. You're helpless."[24]

Evan Galbraith points out that the political process has changed. "To get to the White House you have to make a lot of deals and pay off lots of people."[25] You also have to start running years in advance, like five. Presidential politics is a full-time business, not a part-time avocation.

Plausible reasons, every one, especially Galbraith's: Even sitting politicians have such a hard time winning presidential nominations that the most prudent candidates take care to be out of office or, the next best thing, vice-president. Plausible—and beside the point. Electoral politics was never the strong suit of the Wall Street men. Dewey and Hughes, powerhouse governors, were half-breeds, pols and prosecutors first and foremost, Wall Street lawyers by the way. Wall Street went to Washington when it was picked to go.

Washington, as we have noted, now looks elsewhere. But Wall Street has also sent the signal that it is not interested, and it can't blame its change of mind solely on salaries and confirmations. Yes, you lose money, and yes, the Senate and the *Washington Post* make a formidable tag-team opponent. But what WASP, or WASP-by-adoption, would forsake a duty for such reasons, if he truly felt is as a duty? Civic-mindedness has dropped off Wall Street's agenda—not just the agendas of SEC bogeymen and movie villains, but everyone's.

It may not be, as Stimson feared, that the future of our liberties is gloomy as a result. Perhaps professors and policy nerds will run the State Department as well as Wall Street did. But the future of business is almost certainly gloomier. The commitment to service—even on the part of a tiny minority—served all businessmen as a badge of their worthiness as a class. It was a sign of the rightness of spending all the hours of sunlight in a great business building. It won't be easy to find another.

7

★

Artists in Exile

WASPs, despite their aversion to sensuality, do not have what Mencken called a "libido for the ugly." They can be generous patrons and critics of art. They turn to it for edification—as a cultural acquirement or a source of moral uplift. They can also, when it is willing to present itself comically, turn to it for fun. The crassest WASPs will raid the arts for status symbols—Santayana's candlestick. But art feels different to those who make it: something to be prized of itself, not as a tool in someone else's self-improvement, something more serious than fun (though it is often that too), and certainly more serious than candlesticks. WASPs who create it with more or less good conscience often end up as exiles, actual or internal.

Consider the practitioners of the art in which WASPs have clearly equaled the world, the art of words. Leave aside poets, however neatly Emily Dickinson mured in her house or Ezra Pound free-associating over Italian radio might fit our thesis; most poets everywhere for the last two hundred years have been oddballs. Edgar Allan Poe wrote about no reality observable outside a human skull at three in the morning of a bad night. Professionally he was that saddest of literary creatures, the unsuccessful hack. Nathaniel Hawthorne brooded about the sins of his great-great-grandfather. Washington Irving wrote his best work about New Amsterdam; "Rip Van Winkle" is the most considerable, albeit comic, pro-Tory work in American fiction. Thoreau wrote his best work about a pond. Mark Twain capped a career of journalism and entertainment by becoming, half a century ahead of time, Hal Holbrook. Along the way he wrote two masterpieces in the guise of boys' books, to which he preferred his novel about Joan of Arc. Herman Melville wrote a series of successful South Sea tales, which ended in his masterpiece, slightly less successful. This was followed by the aesthetic and financial disaster of *Pierre* and years of silence. The patriot of American letters turns out, oddly enough, to be Henry James. Isabel Archer and Milly Theal are the subtlest and most perceptive defenses of the American character ever written, greater even than *Democracy in America*. To write them, he spent most of his adult life in London and Paris, and died a British subject and a holder of the Order of Merit. Stephen Crane also got along better in England, where he moved with his companion, a retired brothel-keeper, before dying at the age of twenty-eight. William Faulkner, to push a little farther into the twentieth century, settled himself contentedly, so it seemed, in Oxford, Mississippi (though he drank), writing, so it seemed, about his neighbors and their ancestors (though his characters read more like Joseph Campbell's neighbors).

Comparing these writers to their linguistic cousins, the English masters of roughly the same period, one is immediately struck by the difference—not the difference in quality, for the great WASP writers can hold their heads up in any company, but the difference in subject. From *Sense and Sensibility* to *The Good Soldier,* England produced a stream of books conceived and received as examinations of characters within their social reality. Sometimes the focus was on society, but mostly it was on the characters. Occasionally, as in Dickens, the coloring was garish, hallucinatory. But overall the great English writers showed a rootedness in their surroundings, implying a comfort in their task quite missing in the great WASPs (it is no accident that two of the best of the English were women). The English wrote about their society, and society appreciated the depiction. To imagine an English prose tradition resembling America's, one would have to assume a shift of emphasis whereby the central figures become, say, Wilkie Collins and Rudyard Kipling. In English literature, a work like *Wuthering Heights* stands out as a kind of freak, impressive but solitary. A WASP *Wuthering Heights,* if such a thing could exist, would not stand out at all, for all great WASP writing is freakish. I do not mean to hold up England as a land of happy aesthetes: The spotty history of English painting and the dead end of English music refute that notion. But writing, at least, occurred there with a certain naturalness. Great writers stayed home and wrote about home; the home folks read them; and everybody judged the results with something like accuracy.

There were always WASP writers, of course, plowing the fields of the normal: William Dean Howells, Sinclair Lewis, and so forth and so on. We read them because they fill a gap, but we read them dutifully, because they really don't belong on the first string. Perhaps they wrote as dutifully as we read them. The one top drawer American writer who lived in a WASP social texture and captured it unforgettably was the man who lured George Kennan to Princeton, and he was a lapsed Catholic. *Fitzgerald*

During the last forty years, WASP writers of any kind have grown rarer. The most glittering talents of the postwar generation, and the generation just after, were Jews. Modern American gentiles, the novelist D. Keith Mano has suggested, will be known to future ages in the same way that we know of the Hittites: as background figures in Semitic chronicles. There was also Flannery O'Connor, whose subjects were Southern WASPs but whose perspective was (unlapsed) Catholic, which may explain, though she claimed her intent was ultimately merciful, the batterings to which she subjected them.

Of serious working WASP writers, one thinks of three. There is Louis Auchincloss, picking his way tirelessly through the brownstones; if he did not exist, Digby Baltzell would have to invent him. There is Tom Wolfe, a Southerner who realized he was not condemned at birth to writing only about Sartorises and Misfits and Willie Starks, but that he could get out, raise his head, and look at the entire nation—Southerners (Junior Johnson, Charlie Yeager) included—with distance. If he didn't exist, journalism would have produced something like him, but it wouldn't be as much fun.

Then there is John Updike.

Updike is an interesting case, because he is as normal as Howells; even when he seems to be writing about Africa or ashrams, he keeps circling back to America, like someone looking for a set of keys. Although he denies he is a WASP, as we have seen, the denial is unconvincing, as we shall see.

With all that going against him, he can still write. Line by line, he must be the best American writer alive. Next to his sentences, Mailer's seem at best only lucky, and not all that lucky. Bellow's suggest a shoe salesman, dully stuffing his reader into oxford after oxford that never quite fits. Only Philip Roth's ring as clear. The glory of Updike's sentences is description. Bright little bits of description, thousands of them, are scattered through his fiction, like small but valuable coins—dimes before they took the silver out.

When the sentences cohere in a larger group, as they sometimes do, you feel as if you are zipping down a chute: " . . . in his time Rabbit was famous through the county; in basketball in his junior year he set a B-league scoring record that in his senior year he broke with a record that was not broken until four years later, that is, four years ago."

This sentence appears three pages into *Rabbit, Run,* his second novel. It has been preceded by several bright little bits: "the scrape and snap of Keds" in a boys' basketball game; "the moist March air blue above the wires"; the first shot of Harry "Rabbit" Armstrong, the hero, as he joins in the game, "whipping the net with a ladylike whisper."[1] But the B-league scoring record is what nails us to Rabbit's story. The high point of this man's life was an achievement that stood for four years and is now four years gone. Four and four—still equal, but the second number is only going to get bigger, and there are no more achievements in sight. He is being sucked down.

The hero, as the title suggests, runs. The time of year tempts him, that moist March air. His home, where he arrives after leaving the basketball game, impels him: a cramped, messy walkup where he finds a very pregnant, drunken younger woman, his wife. So, minutes later, does a view, through his parents' kitchen window, of the child he already has, a two-and-a-half-year-old son. He pauses on the sidewalk before entering the house. "The kid cries 'Peel! Peel!': this Rabbit can hear, and understand. It means 'spill.' Pop and Mim [Rabbit's sister] smile and make remarks but Mom, mouth set, comes in grimly with her spoon. Harry's boy is being fed, this home is happier than his. He glides a pace backward over the cement"[2]—and sneaks to the car in which he had meant to drive himself and his son back to his house, and heads out of town.

Rabbit's escape attempt is a smooth, swift curve. The dimes of description—dozens of them: gas stations where he asks directions; an hour of precisely imagined radio programming; the slide of a night getting later and later until it suddenly becomes very early—all slip into place and help propel him along. It is possible to feel, at the outset, that this might be the beginning of a road novel. Kerouac was still in the air when it was published (1960). Updike has said that he intended to answer Kerouac, to show the pain and upheaval that happen when people start hitting the road. At the moment of impact, however, the writer's, and reader's, sympathies are with the runner, if not with his deed, at least with his urge to do something, to find some place where he might once again be a star.

It doesn't work. Trying to take the quickest way south, Rabbit gets lost, then finds himself heading back north, to Pennsylvania. He drives back to his hometown, parks outside the seedy men's club where his old basketball coach lives, and snatches some sleep in the front seat. It is morning.

It would be hard to keep up the clear velocity of these first thirty-five pages, and the rest of the book doesn't. But there are fine things all along the way, enough to make the reader care about Rabbit, and—the ultimate test of realistic fiction—want to know more about him, a desire the author shared, and obliged, in three more novels, eleven, twenty-one, and thirty years later. We're still nailed to his story.

What are the problems? For there are problems. Updike's great virtue, description, can shade alarmingly into a vice. If a character has any sort of special knowledge or skill, from carpentry to computers, grab a lifejacket, for you will be flooded with pedantry. It isn't just specialties that get Updike going. Accepting the American Book Award for *Rabbit Redux,* the second installment of the saga, he confessed that on page 434 he had given Rabbit some clove Life Savers, whereupon a reader wrote to say that there hadn't been a clove flavor for about eight years. "Such are the perils," sighed Updike, "of writing naturalistic fiction."[3] Such, at least, are the perils of writing it when it spins out of control. There are moments when the most graceful stylist in contemporary American letters can be as clotted as Dreiser.

More serious is the problem of shape. Updike's fictions spread like undercooked custards. Sometimes he hits upon a form or a device that imposes control. But since he never seems to learn the lesson, we conclude that the successes were accidental. A smooth sameness—attractive, but uniform nevertheless—glazes everything, recalling the theory that in time matter and energy will be evenly diffused throughout the universe, which will then attain a temperature just above absolute zero. Updike's universe isn't there yet, as a moment like Rabbit's desperation shows, but it's headed that way.

Sex is a more specific, though equally grave problem. Updike did his bit for the revolution in sexual manners and standards that crested in the sixties. The couples in *Couples* (1968) weren't kids, but they were every bit as frisky. And yet Updike can't write an interesting sex scene. There is a willfulness to his characters' copulating that makes scant emotional sense in their own lives and induces no response in the reader. You never know when genitals will appear, though when they do, it is with the air of persistent and vaguely bothersome acquaintances.

Critics—even admiring critics, and most critics of Updike have been admiring—have been harping on these shortcomings for thirty years. The pressure of the way of the WASP, and the need artists have to evade it, helps explain them.

Updike was raised as a Lutheran, and in one self-interview he rejected the term WASP because it implied a different kind of Protestant, a Calvinist. "If the Middle Atlantic states" where he and his characters come from "have a psycho-history," he has said, "it is that Puritanism skipped over them on its way west."[4]

But things aren't so water-tight. "The spirit of Ben Franklin's maxims still lived in the air" of Updike's boyhood, he has testified; they were quoted in his home. One of his grandfathers, ordained as a Presbyterian minister, left his pulpit to sell insurance and real estate, and failed—and took it like a Presbyterian. "In my mythic sense of my family the stain of unsuccess ate away at my grandfather's life as if in some tale by Hawthorne."[5] Hero after Updike hero—Joey Robinson, Richard Maple, Piet Hanema, Rabbit—confronted with material or moral disorder, reaches for the same word to express his horror and dismay: *waste*. What WASPier pejorative could there be?

Updike tried to escape, not by car but by the means favored by many a discontented WASP, a new religion. The escape was a subtle one, for the new religion he found as a young adult—the theology of the German Swiss theologian Karl Barth—presented itself as a return to orthodoxy.

Barth, a pastor in the Reformed (Calvinist) Church, had been engaged, since the early twenties, in an effort to haul German Protestant theology back to dogma. "Only those," wrote Barth's first translator into English, "who are old enough to remember the particular kind of desiccated humanism, almost empty of other-worldly content, which prevailed in many Protestant areas in the early decades of this century, can understand the surprise, the joy, the refreshment" Barth brought.[6] Updike, for a time anyway, understood and shared them. Halfway through *Rabbit, Run,* Rev. Eccles (Episcopalian), who ministers to Rabbit's in-laws, tries to consult with Rev. Kruppenbach (Lutheran), the pastor of the Angstroms' church. Updike gives the Lutheran a fine Barthian blast. "I say you don't know what your role is or you'd be home locked in prayer. *There* is your role: to make yourself an exemplar of faith. *There* is where comfort comes from: faith, not what little finagling a body can do here and there."[7] Justification by faith alone, as another Lutheran remarked. By way of Switzerland, Updike came home to Luther after all, and got some theological purchase on non-WASP ground.

But there is a problem. On inspection, Barth's version of orthodoxy turns out to be peculiar. His faith leads to less than Luther's. In 1963, three years after *Rabbit Run, The New Yorker,* "out of deference to my curious habit, Christianity," let Updike review a dense, recently translated work by Barth examining the ontological proof of God's existence by the eleventh-century theologian Anselm. The ontological proof, Updike explained, "makes no appeal to the natural world." It is an intellectual maneuver that seeks to deduce God by definition. Many philosophers, some Christian (Aquinas), some not (Kant), have had problems with it. Barth endorsed it; what other proof could a theologian of pure faith accept? But, as Updike discovered with some dismay, he accepted it as a description of a God in whose existence we already believe: *If* God exists, then Anselm's depiction of Him is accurate. Barth accepted the proof, in short, even though to his mind it proved nothing. But "such, we must weakly confess," Updike wrote, was "the proof that we had hoped for." In raising God beyond attack, Barth lifted Him beyond contact. "We cannot reach Him," as Updike put it. "Only He can reach us."[8] A dozen years later, another one of Updike's clergymen puts it more harshly. (He is talking with a colleague, with whom he shares a lover—just so we're sure these are Updike clergymen.) "This terrible absolute unknowable other. It panders to despair."[9]

We do not know—Updike's *Memoirs* are reticent—to what sort of despair Barth may have pandered in his own life, and as readers we shouldn't want to know. We can see the effects on, or at least the fit with, his fiction. Once the inescapable facts that usually preoccupy beginning writers—parents, childhood, adolescence—have been used, what remains, to the God's eye, especially if the God is

Barth's? From such a remote height, what can human lives look like, except an undifferentiated and disorganized dailiness, which happens to be the stuff—the clogging stuff—of Updike's fiction? Updike loves dailiness; he has claimed as his mission the task of preserving and evoking it. But dailiness isn't enough. If it were, all we would need to write, and read, would-be diaries. The only mundane thing that stands up from the plane of the God-flattened world is sex. It gets author and characters going, if not readers. So Updike falls back on it compulsively.

Antisensuality, as it inhibits art, may be the toughest article of the way of the WASP to overturn. It is easy to confute or resist an exhortation. You simply ignore it. A prohibition can also be ignored. But it is harder to build up positive interior encouragement in its place. John Updike wants to be an artist, and he wants, terminological quibbles aside, to remain a normal, everyday WASP. He has had, as a result, a hard row to hoe. He seemed to make it easier for himself by making a small but significant mental escape into an eccentric brand of Protestantism. But he doesn't seem to be very happy with it, and it drains rather than energizes his fiction. All he has, finally, is his talent to help him. Fortunately, that is considerable; for, in a WASP world, talent has an uphill struggle, against an unusually steep hill.

Another art in which America has clearly excelled has been music, though WASPs have not excelled in it. The first notable American composer was Johann Caspar Friedrich, a Moravian immigrant to eighteenth-century Pennsylvania, who wrote some pleasant chamber music. He set the pattern.

From Louis Moreau Gottschalk to Louis Armstrong, from Leon Bismarck Beiderbecke to Leonard Bernstein, good American music has been overwhelmingly the work of non-WASPs—Germans, Jews, blacks. We remember WASP individuals here and there—William Billings, Cole Porter—and, less often, whole styles of WASP music, such as the white half of rock 'n' roll. The rest is silence.

It's hard, without an understanding of the way of the WASP, to explain why this should be so. There were no outright prohibitions on music-making. American Protestantism is a singing religion. WASPs have made excellent audiences for other people's tunes. The first performance of *Parsifal* outside Bayreuth was at the Met in New York. A special train carried Wagnerites in from Chicago for the occasion. They like popular music too: However much jazz musicians like to think of themselves as a gloomy and lonely coterie, if no one but themselves listened, they would all have to prepare tax forms for a living.

Antisensuality is the creative damper. The mental habits of WASPs, which forced them to create great fiction obliquely, half-consciously, or rebelliously, with difficulty, prevented them, with few exceptions, from creating great music at all. The greatest exception was Charles Ives, whose strange career, so normal and yet so isolated—so normal, and therefore so isolated—confirms the rule.

I had heard some Charles Ives before 1974. My high school band had played his undeservedly popular stunt piece, "Variations on 'America'"—a Mexican version, a version in minor, and so on—but the year of his centennial represented an apotheosis, during which he was inescapable. Nowhere was he less escapable than Yale.

Ives had gone to Yale in the class of '98, ten years after Henry Stimson, a few years before Dink Stover. He had taken music courses there, but he hadn't much liked them. Horatio Parker, the head of the Yale music department, made him normalize the last movement of his First Symphony, his senior project. The symphony was normal enough anyway, and pretty uninspired. Seventy-six years after his graduation, Yale was determined to make it up to him.

At times it went overboard. There was one trying Ivesian half-time show at a football game, in which the Whiffenpoofs were perplexedly involved. They even resurrected the First Symphony. "All those themes," Fenno Heath, the director of the Glee Club and a pupil of Hindemith, remarked during a rehearsal, as the Brahmsian melodies sturdily presented themselves, "all those themes, and nothing happens to them." But most of what I was able to perform was rich and strange, out of Ives's top drawer, or anyone's—the 67th Psalm, the 90th Psalm, a haunting heard-in-the-mind's-ear hymn arrangement, "Shall We Gather at the River?"

The Ives revival provoked one small dispute, which was, oddly enough, political. The Glee Club was learning a unison arrangement of "They Are There!" a patriotic song Ives first wrote in World War I then updated for World War II. The music was engagingly loony: snippets of popular and patriotic melodies—"Columbia, Gem of the Ocean," "Tenting Tonight," "Rally 'Round the Flag"—strung together into one long boisterous tune. "He tried

to get me to sing it," a nephew of Ives recalled years later. "There
was one little passage which called for a real shout, but I shouted
very timidly and he nearly hit the roof. 'Can't you shout better than
that? That's the trouble with this country—people are afraid to
shout!'"[10] The problem was not the tune or the shout but the words,
which Ives had written himself. Some members of the Glee Club
objected to their bumptiousness. They were certainly bumptious.

> When we're through this cursed war
> All started by a sneaky gouger,
> Making slaves of men . . .

The song looked forward to "a people's brand-new world," but only
after "the allies beat up all the war-hogs." At post-Vietnam, post-
Watergate Yale, the objectors held, such sentiments lacked *ton*.

The song's defenders made two arguments: (1) art for art's sake.
Geniuses can say anything they like, though I doubt we would have
extended this privilege to, say, Céline. More important, (2) we
shouldn't take the song literally. We are all sophisticates, so was
Ives. Surely the song was an ironic reflection of popular sentiments,
not a sincere rant about war-hogs. It had been written in quotes, as
it were; certainly that was how we would sing it. Let's not miss the
joke.

We ended up not doing it, which was a pity. But the joke was on its
defenders, for the song was quite sincere.

Ives was born on Main Street in Danbury, Connecticut. His father,
the town bandmaster, was ever on the lookout for new sounds.
Different bands playing different tunes simultaneously interested
him enormously. "The people in Danbury didn't think it was very
interesting," a family friend commented years later.[11] He also listened to nature. "One afternoon in a pouring thunderstorm," Ives
himself wrote, "we saw him standing without hat or coat in the back
garden; the church bell next door was ringing. He would rush into
the house to the piano, and then back again. 'I've heard a chord I've
never heard before—it comes over and over but I can't seem to
catch it.' He stayed up most of the night trying to find it in the
piano."[12] Ives, in adult life, was not quite as isolated from contemporary music as he is sometimes depicted. He had heard "The
Firebird" (and found it repetitious), and some Debussy and Ravel.
In his later years, after he had stopped actively composing, he was

seen with a Prokofiev score on his desk. But his search for new sounds began in Danbury.

Another influence on Ives was the crowd that had looked down on the Adamses: Concord. The Concord literati and illuminati were constantly on his mind. The movements of Ives's Second piano sonata are named after Emerson, Hawthorne, the Alcotts, and Thoreau. Ives was sustained in his interest by the dense texture of New England life, which could be as incestuous as the South. His grandmother had heard Emerson speak in Danbury; one of his nieces once played "the Alcotts" movement of the Concord sonata on Louisa May Alcott's piano. Ives's admiration of these looming predecessors was notably innocent; his understanding of them was in general morally superior to the originals. He took from Thoreau, for example, not the hatred of humanity nor the imperfectly suppressed bloodlust, but the love of nature, especially of natural sounds. "At a sufficient distance over the woods," Thoreau had written in *Walden,* the sound of a church bell "acquires a certain vibratory hum, as if the pine needles in the horizon were the strings of a harp which it swept."[13] From Emerson he took, not self-deification, but a pleasure in elevated thoughts. His Hawthorne is not a post-Puritan gloomster, but a fantasist. Ives stayed closer to the faith of his fathers than any of them: so close that his disciple and exegete, John Kirkpatrick, could call him "almost" a "Fundamentalist." "He was almost in a state of 'Give me that old-time religion, it's good enough for me.'"[14]

Ives did not lack for peculiarities of his own, however. He had a lifelong interest in politics, which he expressed in privately printed pamphlets and letters to editors and famous people, which were just a cut above the stuff that comes in nowadays triple-underlined, in green ink, with PSes spilling over onto the envelope. He devised a scheme for constitutional amendments that provided for referendums on federal legislation, and he believed that the whole world might be run under such a system, once war-hogs and sneaky gougers had been disposed of. The only serious response Ives ever got from any of his famous correspondents was from former president Taft, who counted himself "very much opposed" to Ives's amendment plan. "It is impracticable, and would much change the form of our Government."[15]

Ives's populism took a more realistic form in his workaday career, which was insurance. He constructed one of the first systems for rationally calculating the amount of insurance a consumer ought to carry, based on income and expenses. (When I bought insurance recently, I asked the agent if he knew Ives's pamphlet, "The Amount to Carry." He had heard of it. He had no idea that Ives had been a composer.) He viewed his formula as a way of diffusing necessary knowledge. "The Minority Mind," he wrote (he liked capital letters), "has been too timid to trust the Majority Mind, and hence reluctant to pass around the 'facts.'"[16]

Yet his music remained a Minority taste. Ives composed feverishly from the 1890s through the teens; fear of an early death, like his father's at forty-nine, spurred him on. In 1918 he had a serious heart attack, after which he wrote little that was new, though he continued to revise old pieces, often substantially. Ives had his admirers, and there were performances of his music in Berlin, Budapest, and Paris—where "Three Places in New England" became *Trois Coins de Nouvelle Angleterre*—as well as America, now and again during the twenties and thirties. One Ives lover tried to get the Budapest Quartet to play his first string quartet. They refused on the grounds that it was "just a lot of cheap American religious music."

> That got me irritated and I said, "Well, it is no different from Haydn." They said, "What do you mean? Haydn is a great composer." I said, "Yeah, but there were cheap beer garden tunes in his quartets." They said, "Oh, that's different." And I said, "No, it isn't different. You don't mind them, but you mind these. That's all."[17]

The Budapest didn't bite.

The perfect *mitteleuropaisch* counterpart of Ives, as foil, not soulmate, is Gustav Mahler. Compare some bit of Ives with the famous posthorn solo in the third movement of Mahler's Third Symphony. Formally, there are a number of resemblances: a quoted melody inflected by distance or memory; a touch of nostalgia; even the penchant for elaborate philosophizing programs. But how different the music actually is, and how much credit the difference reflects on the American. Musically, Mahler's posthorn—and his Frère Jacques funeral march from the First Symphony, and his tedious Austrian dances from every symphony—are unimaginative and simple-minded. Ives knows that time, space, dreaming, or excitement distort the music that passes through them. To convey these distortions, he reaches for bold sonic effects, ranging from melodic missteps to outright noise.

Ives's breakthrough was a performance by Kirkpatrick of the Concord Sonata at Town Hall in New York in 1939; it had taken Kirkpatrick ten years to get the work ready. Premieres of major pieces trickled on through the forties and fifties, and Ives was awarded a Pulitzer at the age of seventy-three. The Fourth Symphony was first performed in its entirety in 1965, eleven years after Ives had died.

One source of Ives's vogue, when it finally came, was this aura of almost universal incomprehension in which he had worked. So the avant-garde, we like to think, suffers everywhere. Yet Ives's career was different from that of other misunderstood modernists. He was no bohemian. In some ways, he came the closest of all American artists—certainly all WASP artists—to leading a normal life. He wrote about things he had heard and felt in his daily experience. He held a responsible and remunerative job, which harmonized with his philosophy. He was as grounded as Trollope. The only difference was that hardly anyone liked his music. "So why don't you compose something pretty, Charlie?" his brother would tease him. Physically and spiritually, Ives stayed at home. Home ignored him—just as home had ignored his father. "They didn't take Ives [senior] very seriously," added the old friend who recalled Danbury's lack of interest in unsynchronized stereo. "He was only a bandleader."[18]

There was talk, in the sixties, that Ives might be the fount of an American modernism. As the first half of the century belonged to Schoenberg and Stravinsky, the second would belong to Bartók and Ives.[19] It hasn't happened. The best American music, since Ives stopped actively composing, has been the popular music whose earlier expressions he mined so diligently, music that evades the prohibitions against taking art seriously because it offers itself as entertainment. Ives tried to live a serious musical life at the heart of WASP culture. But he was rejected, as a body rejects a transplant, and taken up, in his old age and after his death, as a fad.

Am I wrong to remember a certain self-consciousness to Yale's Ives year? a whiff of camp? a hint of pop? The jacket of the record of the Fourth Symphony I bought around then captures it perfectly. The cover illustration shows a Primitive statue standing in a field, draped with bunting: Our Sturdy Past. The difference between what Ives thought he was up to and what we did was the difference between America and Americana.

There will come a time, for good and ill, when the "cheap American religious music" the Budapest complained of will be as culturally neutral in a listener's ears as the "cheap beer garden tunes" of Haydn are now. What will remain will be sensual and structural pleasures: simple melodies, subtly bent, and merging or clashing masses of sound.

While the associations are still fading, the feeling they induce is one of pathos. Ives himself had an inkling of this. The nephew who wouldn't shout loud enough remembered a rare visit Ives paid in his later years to Danbury (as an adult he lived in New York and in West Redding, Connecticut). "I went out walking with him late that evening, and we went up as far as the Civil War monument in the City Hall Square. . . . He actually moaned aloud when he got there and saw how it had all changed. . . . And he turned around and went back to the old house and said he was sorry he had gone out at all."[20]

The first two-thirds of the 90th Psalm, for mixed chorus and organ, the only work, according to his wife, that satisfied him, is a feast of complexities—rude parallel fourths, tone clusters, grotesque voice leading, with two sweet solos for tenor and soprano thrown in, all appropriate to the general tone of the text: "For all our days are passed away in thy wrath, we spend our years as a tale that is told." A four-measure introduction lays out the basic chords and assigns them names: The Eternities, Creation, God's wrath against sin, Prayer and Humility, Rejoicing in Beauty and Work. Moments of it are almost unlearnably perverse; I never quite got the fourths. Then, at measure 93, mercy breaks in; singers and organ are joined by bells ("as church bells, in distance" Ives writes in the score), and the piece ends with a long, Amen-like stretch in C major—there is still a lot of good music to be written in C major, Schoenberg said—though the bells, slowly and more slowly, continue to slip in mild, melting sharps, like swept pine needles.

> And let the beauty of the Lord our God be upon us:
> and establish thou the work of our hands upon us;
> yea, the work of our hands establish thou it.

Their days passed away; it was not established.

8

*

Losing the Faith

*O*UT MY BEDROOM WINDOW I have a view of the towers of
St. George's Episcopal Church. It is a brown Romanesque
Revival building, a national historical landmark, finished in 1856,
rebuilt after a fire nine years later. A Stuyvesant donated the land
on which it stands. In the nineteenth century the towers supported
steeples, but when they were found to be structurally unsound,
they were removed. The towers now look squarishly over a small
park, recently reclaimed from drug dealers and homosexual pros-
titutes.

St. George's is famous chiefly for having been the church of J. P.
Morgan. Morgan, who made a youthful hobby of collecting the
signatures of Episcopàlian bishops, grew up to be a devout churchman. His career as a mogul and as an Episcopalian coincided with
what Baltzell called "the Episcopalianization of the American business aristocracy."[1] Morgan first learned of the crash of 1907, which
he managed to stem with his own financial and political clout, while
attending a General Convention of the Episcopal Church in Rich-
mond, where he had come in two special railroad cars in the
company of four bishops, three American and one English. Morgan served as the senior warden of St. George's, a position he nearly
resigned when the rector put a working man on the parish board.
Morgan believed in democratizing the church but wanted the ves-
try "to remain a body of gentlemen whom I can ask to meet me in
my study."[2] Morgan ultimately accepted the working vestryman
and stayed on. Alfred Thayer Mahan, the naval historian, did
resign.

St. George's and the Episcopal Church in New York City gener-

97

ally were not just about money and power. The democratic rector, W. S. Rainsford, had come from England, where he had been a follower of the Christian Socialism movement. Rainsford's bishop, Henry Codman Potter, also a friend of Morgan, was the second president of the Church Association for the Advancement of the Interests of Labor and a respected strike arbitrator. Socialism, at the same time, did not preclude social standing. In the Episcopal Church of those days, good intentions and good breeding went hand in hand. "Wherever [Potter] went, he entered naturally, as by right, into the best society. It was a matter of course that at Baden-Baden he walked with the Prince of Wales, and that in London . . . he was sought out by the Archbishop of Canterbury."[3]

That was then. The symbol of the Episcopal Church in New York City today, or at least of the church as its leaders wish to present it, is the Cathedral of St. John the Divine, a hundred blocks north on the West Side. The cornerstone was laid in 1892, during the the episcopacy of Henry Potter, and it has been growing at a leisurely pace ever since. St. John commands what is, by Manhattan standards, an enormous tract of ground—11½ acres. Architecturally it is one of the finest churches in New York, certainly the finest large church. St. Patrick's, the Roman Catholic cathedral in midtown, is a lot of fun. St. John inspires awe. But if God is in the details, one must look beyond the immensity.

As in most cathedrals, the walls of St. John are lined with chapels. One June afternoon, I made a circuit of the nave to see what was being memorialized. Some of the displays were genuinely moving, the most moving being a pair of crossed, charred spars in memory of twelve "heroic firefighters" who died battling a blaze on 23d Street in 1966. A billed cap, bearing the name of an engine company, lay on the spot: homage. Nearby was a chapel containing commemorations of the Armenian massacres and the Holocaust, whose effectiveness was slightly diminished by being placed together, as if some tidy-minded memorialist of disaster had accomplished a twofer.

Other exhibits were harder to take. There was, here and there, the Anglophile chic that non-Episcopalians find so baffling: a notice that a motherhood window, in memory of a van Renssalaer, had been unveiled in 1954 by "Her Majesty Queen Elizabeth the Queen Mother." Dean Acheson's father would have liked it, but what do the Yanks think? England, however, has been superseded in Episcopalian affections by Earth. There was an Earth Shrine, dedicated to Francis of Assisi and displaying a picture of him preaching to the wolf of Gubbio, which is at least a Christian story (the saint persuaded the wolf to stop his depredations). But there was also a sculpture, by one of the cathedral's artists-in-residence, of a wolf in all its bristly, unreconstructed wolfishness (if Nature is good, why does it require preachment?). Beside the wolf sat a huge fossilized shell, neatly labeled "100 million year old ammonite from New Mexico."

Soon everything started running together: a stone effigy of William Thomas Manning, tenth Bishop of New York; next to it a 2,000-pound quartz crystal from Arkansas. There was a sleek, craftsy wooden table supporting a Japanese flower arrangement. Above it hung a "banner of Humankind," consisting of black, brown, red, white, and yellow stripes—plus green, for the "one earth, sustainer of all." Across from it stood a crucifix painted with pictures of murdered Nicaraguan peasants; one had a stars-and-stripes dagger handle protruding from her breast. A posted prayer for the safety of Terry Waite, the mediator missing in Lebanon, caused a shock. Waite worked for the Archbishop of Canterbury; wasn't praying for one of your own a bit *narrow?* On the way out was a Poet's Corner, dedicated to American literature, which had gotten as far as Robert Frost.

A map of the complex showed that there was a Biblical Garden back on the cathedral's south side. This was an older style of devotion, fantasy and edification mixed: See the plants the Savior saw. I sat on a bench out of the sun. Also escaping the heat were four peacocks, a blue-green blaze. They were a long way from Galilee.

The impulse to lead, in socially correct ways, was still there, as were the trappings of power. But the white Protestant churches that had made the most political and social impact on the seventies and the eighties were not the St. John the Divines, but those on the opposite end of the Protestant spectrum, ideologically and ceremonially. Later in the month I visited the Thomas Road Baptist church of Lynchburg, Virginia, the church of Jerry Falwell, founder of the Moral Majority and symbol, for a few years at least, of the religious right.

For all New Yorkers know, Lynchburg is Tobacco Road. In fact, it is a factory city in the foothills of the Appalachians, a place where people get drawn into the larger world. Sometimes to their disadvantage: CRACK GANGS INVADE LYNCHBURG was the head-

line of *The News & Daily Advance* the day I was there. A sign blocking
the entrance to the church parking lot said it was full, use the lot
across the street. The backup lot already had a hundred cars in it.
License plates from half a dozen states greeted me as I passed. Most
of them probably belonged to students at Liberty Baptist, Falwell's
college, but others marked the cars of travelers who had made a
point to come here, as to Monticello. The church, which had held its
first services in an old bottling plant, now occupied a huge brick
split-level with two porticoes. How many worshipers do you expect?
I asked an usher inside. Oh, it was summer, he said, so they would
be down: maybe as low as 2,500.

Falwell's services are broadcast as the *Old Time Gospel Hour,* and
portable cameras slid smoothly through the sanctuary as the hour
unfolded. But it was still a service, recognizably like all the other
services of American Protestantism, apart from the most elaborate
Anglo-Catholicism or the plainest faith-healing. Falwell's delivery
was earnest and level, no Swaggart showing. There was Bach during the offertory; the plate, I noticed, was passed before the sermon, as Methodists do, and not after, like Presbyterians and Congregationalists, when it gives the feeling of a judgment on services
rendered. The hymn book was heavy with the standbys of Charles
Wesley and Isaac Watts. The performed music was familiar from
other contexts: brassy, overproduced, grating, as bad as music at
political conventions, indeed, bad for the same reason—it is a
producer's notion of what sounds upbeat over television. It was a
trial to endure it live. At one point a quartet of singers did a break in
scat. I thought of Ives's father: "When [he] had choruses, he used
men to sing who were way off pitch. People made fun of this, but
he'd say, 'What of it? They have the spirit of it.'" I also thought,
abashedly, of one of Updike's ministers. "Is not our distate here
aesthetic, where aesthetics are an infernal category?"[4]

The service was of more than usual interest, for Falwell had
announced earlier in the week that he was closing down the Moral
Majority, the organization he had ridden to fame, and notoriety, in
1979, and his sermon was an explication of his new course. He
maintained that it was not new. He had never been primarily an
evangelist, he said, much less a televangelist, but rather a pastor.
Continuing as a pastor and a church planter was his goal for the
next fifteen years. "As young people say it, where it's at is the local
church." He recalled his own years as a young minister, when he
had hung a map of Lynchburg on his church office wall, marking

out a ten-block radius labeled Jerusalem, a twenty-block radius Judea, and a thirty block radius Samaria. He had knocked on every door in those hopeful circles and, ultimately, every door in all of Lynchburg. "That is how we can change the world in our genera- tion—by planting thousands of new churches in this country that believe in the Bible and win souls for Christ." How do we save the cities? "Weep and pray over our cities. That's how Jesus did it." He had wept over Lynchburg. "Nothing does Satan hate more than the planting of a local Bible-preaching church." He ended with a call for anyone who was not born again to come down the aisle. The hour was up, the cameras went off. Outside, on Thomas Road, three cops directed the departing traffic.

The founder of the religious right had come full circle. He was still concerned to change the world. But the primary means would no longer be political agitation, but through the work of active churches. It was, curiously, a path not unlike that being followed by New York's Episcopalians. Except that one church embodied old- fashioned swank and New Age rock worship, while the other repre- sented fundamentalism.

American Protestantism, the keeper of the WASP conscience, today suffers from a schism. St. John the Divine and Thomas Road Baptist display it in extreme form, though still more extreme con- trasts could easily be presented. American Protestants are not new to squabbles. In the seventeenth century they occasionally hanged each other. In the nineteenth century the slavery question split the major WASP denominations in half. Like the Civil War, the schism of today cuts across denominations, as well as between them. Like other conflicts, it involves matters of belief and behavior. But this schism is the most serious, for it has been growing for a hundred years. One side—St. John the Divine—sees itself as theologically and culturally sophisticated, the other—Thomas Road Baptist—is seen as primitive. There is enough of the dirt of truth in that to support the pearl of distortion. But it is the self-styled sophisticates who have strayed from the way of the WASP. At issue is the cultural control of American Protestantism, and hence, indirectly, of Amer- ican life.

The parties to the split are often characterized as the mainline versus an enemy with no settled name—sideline would be frivo- lous—though the terms "evangelical" and "fundamentalist" are commonly, and misleadingly, pressed into service.* The mainline, in this scheme, is the historical Protestant establishment—"the channel of continuity . . . of American religious experience since the seventeenth century," as Richard John Neuhaus puts it, "the churches that many Americans view as 'standard brand' religion— Presbyterian, Methodist, Episcopalian, Congregationalist."[5]

This denominational lineup blurs a number of historical and social realities. The Presbyterians, Episcopalians, and Congregationalists (now the United Church of Christ) are among the three oldest Protestant churches in America, and for most of the eighteenth century they were the largest. Methodism, by contrast, was a late starter. John Wesley, its English founder, made one visit to the colonies, which was a failure. During the Revolution he urged his American followers to remain loyalists. Once Methodism took root, though, it grew rapidly until, by the 1840s, it had become the largest church in America. Yet it was never a church of the elite. Theodore Roosevelt once said he would "rather address a Methodist audience than any other" because they "represent the great middle class."[6] Presidents of the United States might have wanted to address Methodists; it is unlikely that J. P. Morgan would have.

A subtler denominational breakdown, proposed by two sociologists, Wade Clark Roof and William McKinney, arranges white American Protestantism in three groups: liberals (Episcopalians, Presbyterians, United Church of Christ), conservatives (Southern Baptists, Churches of Christ, Assemblies of God, Nazarenes), and moderates. Under the moderate rubric, Roof and McKinney place Methodists, Disciples of Christ, Northern Baptists, Lutherans, and members of Reformed churches, not because of any doctrinal or historical kinship—there is none—but for common sociological factors: "fairly sizable constituencies . . . a similar social location, and . . . middle American values and outlook."[7]

Denominational lumping is a useful way to sift and compare the figures, but it misses dissension within denominations. The Southern Baptists have been engaged in a years-long struggle between

---

*Evangelicals believe in the necessity of a transforming commitment to a Christian life. Fundamentalists affirm the inerrancy of the Bible. Charismatics believe that prophetic gifts described in the New Testament, such as speaking in tongues, occur today. All fundamentalists are evangelicals, but the reverse is not true. Fundamentalists and charismatics don't much like each other: Charistmatics tend to find fundamentalists pharisaical, while fundamentalists suspect charismatics of paying insufficient attention to Scripture. Charismatics exist in all American Christian churches, not just WASP ones.

fundamentalists and liberals. When the Episcopal Church ordained its first woman bishop, a radical lesbian with no pastoral
experience, disgruntled bishops formed a conservative Synod
within the church. Presbyterians and Methodists each have small
dissident movements. Apart from organized politicking, there are
simply broad differences of sentiment among believers. Most believers probably don't care, because they rarely run into their
opposite numbers. Contact might be traumatic: It would be hard to
imagine the Episcopalian George Bush praying before a Sandinista
cross.

In the past, when differences yawned and passions rose, dissatisfied Protestants would pull out of the church they were in and set
up something new. King's Chapel kept its chaunts, but not the Holy
Ghost. Today the notion of a church reorganizing itself because of a
doctrinal differences seems quaint. The fights simmer within denominations. Each side of the schism feels that it is legitimate. Why
leave when you are already where you belong and when it is the
other guy who should admit that he has strayed?

The schism itself is often described, in the supposedly neutral
language of social science, as the result of Protestantism's encounter with modernity, the liberals embracing it, conservatives resist-
ing, though this stacks the deck. Since modernity, literally speaking, is as inevitable as the next page of the calendar, how can anyone
sensibly resist it? The institutions which keep the WASP conscience
are split, more precisely, as a result of their encounters with three
things.

The first disruptive force was the higher criticism, the application,
especially in Germany, of historical and textual analysis to the Bible,
as to any other ancient document. The project, which is ongoing, at
the very least modified traditional accounts of how various texts
came to be written and transmitted. At its most extreme it abolished
the accounts—and the texts as well.

The arcana of scholars was bound to hit Protestantism hard,
because it is a religion of the book. The ultimate forum of choice, as
we said earlier, is still the conscience. But no American Protestants,
except Quakers, would rely on it apart from the instructions and
injunctions of the Bible. The Book, as Dean Acheson remarked,
was all.

Higher criticism hit Protestants doubly hard because of their
aversion to theology. Methodists, again, are symptomatic here:

" . . . from real Christians, of whatever *denomination*," John Wesley once wrote, "I earnestly desire not to be distinguished at all. . . . Dost thou love and fear God? It is enough! I give thee the right hand of fellowship."[8] This sentiment would have a natural appeal in America. Theology, like any other form of speculation, risks failing the test of use. Why quibble when there is a job—living the Christian life—to be done, and the way to do it seems so clear? The result of scanting theology is that it is not there when it is needed. Theology, after all, is simply a way of sorting out the truths and facts of religion and the world. Confronted with a redating of Biblical texts, which places them years beyond the lifetimes of their traditional authors, the theologian asks the essential next question: So what? What do we make of this?—to which there will be a range of possible answers. The nontheologian must either ignore the difficulty or stubbornly defend his old belief. Or, in the worst case, accept the tacit premise of the redater, that the texts are somehow debunked.

For there was a will to debunk in much of the higher criticism, and many American Protestants, like police dogs, sniffed it quite plainly. It is no accident, for example, that the dates the first wave of German scholars assigned to the Gospels were decades later than what scholarship now accords them. The disposition to complicate questions of authorship—to look "behind" presumed revisions for minimalist *ur*-texts—was itself theological. German theology of the early nineteenth century was hot to pare Christianity down to essences, rational or romantic. What the philosophers of religion wanted, the scholars obligingly discovered.

American Protestantism, so little encumbered by theology, had trouble absorbing the shock. Just as the political progressives would tear the public functions of the conscience away from principles that were "rounded, perfect, ideal," so the new theology cut religious conscience loose from its scriptural moorings. The Protestant response tended to be all or nothing. Rather, all or anything—redated John to the death of God in a hundred years.

The second disruptive force was the Social Gospel. Protestants had never been shy about attacking specific evils. Abolition was a religious crusade. Earlier in the nineteenth century, Protestants North and South campaigned successfully against the practice of dueling. By the end of the century, however, big industries and big cities seemed to present an interrelated complex of vices, which required nothing less than an attempt to reform society as a whole.

It should be noted that, at the intellectual level, the Social Gospel was a reaction. The vogue immediately preceding it had been Social Darwinism. Henry Ward Beecher's thoughts on the poor have already been cited. William Graham Sumner, the academic free marketeer, was a lapsed Episcopalian minister, much as forty years later the socialist politician Norman Thomas would be a lapsed Presbyterian minister.

We have seen how the next wave reached the Episcopalian upper class. The main channel of diffusion to average clergymen was Walter Rauschenbusch, a Baptist minister from Rochester, New York, and son of a German immigrant, whose turning point came when he was assigned in the 1880s to a parish abutting Hell's Kitchen in New York City. Two decades later he published *Christianity and the Social Crisis*. But the most popular sermon on the new gospel was Charles Sheldon's *In His Steps*.

In His Steps has sold 30 million copies since the 1890s, and it still sells today, though it can be hard to find. One afternoon, as an experiment, I went down Fifth Avenue looking for a copy. I even cut over to a Logos bookstore on Madison, a Christian chain heavy on the Inklings. They had Dr. Robertiello on WASPs, but not *In His Steps*. A few months later I was in Johnstown, New York (pop. 9,300), visiting relatives. On the main street, which is called Main Street, was a small Christian bookstore. They had it.

In His Steps shows how ambiguous the radicalism of the Social Gospel was, at least at the popular level. The book describes (with no skill) what happens in a fictional Midwestern town (Charles Sheldon was a Congregationalist minister in Topeka, Kansas) and in Chicago when Christians take a pledge to do nothing in their daily lives without first asking, "What would Jesus do?" What happens is, with one exception, not particularly political. At one point in the story a Single Taxer, a Trade Unionist, and a Socialist (with the immigrant name of Carlsen; every other surname in the book is pure WASP) make pitches for their creeds. The only purpose of the scene is to make the hero reflect that social ills would not be so desperate, and the church would not be so hated by radicals, if only all Christians lived like Jesus. For employers, this means running their business on some (unspecified) principle of "cooperation." One character, a newspaper editor, kills his Sunday edition and stops carrying accounts of crimes and boxing matches. Another character, at the cost of his job, turns the local railroad in to the Interstate Commerce Commission for giving special treatment to favored shippers. There is even a writer who realizes that, as a novelist, "Jesus would use His powers to produce something useful or helpful, or with a purpose." He doesn't, and embarks on the road to Hell. All the "good" characters make considerable sacrifices of time and money to work in slum settlement houses. The one time they unite at the polls is to shut down the saloons. The effort fails. "O Lord God," writes the author in his own voice, "how long, how long?"[9]

The dry politicking apart, there is little here, in other words, that goes beyond traditional good works. Significantly, *In His Steps* has been brought out, for the nth time, by the Word Press of Dallas, one of the country's largest suppliers of evangelical and fundamentalist books—by the heirs, in other words, of those who rejected the Social Gospel as an innovation—with no sense of cognitive dissonance.

But the Social Gospel impulse could, and did, take programmatic political forms. After the Bethlehem Steel strike of 1910, the recently formed Federal Council of Churches declared the twelve-hour day and the seven-day week "a disgrace to civilization," an unexceptionable criticism nowadays. But its political hopes also came clothed in a rhetoric of millennial expectation. If only the "economic and intellectual resources of humanity" could be harnessed to good, wrote Rauschenbusch in the peroration of his big book, the "great day of the Lord for which the ages waited" would begin. Even *In His Steps* ends, more humbly but no less confidently, with a prayer for the "dawn of the millennium of Christian history."[10] One consequence of such notions was a devaluation of industry and success, even when the Social Gospelers did not assail them directly. Preaching the millennium, however vaguely, cannot encourage people to spend ten hours a day in an office. These heaven-on-earth hopes meanwhile remained in the soil of American Protestantism, ready to bud at various seasons for various purposes.

American Protestantism's last moment of political and social unity did not reflect much credit on it. This was Prohibition.[11] Sheldon's Christians, following in Jesus' steps, finally won their vote. Methodists played a major role. Frances Willard, founder of the Women's Christian Temperance Union, which also crusaded for women's suffrage and against prostitution, called herself "a strictly loyal and orthodox Methodist." The Anti-Saloon League, which finally put Prohibition in the Constitution, was organized nationally by a Methodist minister. But all WASP Protestantism pitched in. The religious and ethnic cast of the campaign—"besodden Europe," went a typical tract, "sends here her drink-makers, her drunkard-makers, and her drunkards . . . with all their un-American and anti-American ideas"—was enough to drive dry Irish Catholics out of the temperance movement. It did not impede its success at the polls. Success in practice was another matter. Repeal, when it came, was "the greatest blow to their pride and self-confidence that Protestants as a collective body had ever experienced."[12]

The New Deal ought to have revived the spirits of the activist wing. One member of the Federal Council of Churches praised the federal government for "applying many of the policies which the churches had advocated for two decades." Some Protestant publications indeed criticized Roosevelt from the left. In 1934 a Methodist youth group circulated a pledge which began: "I surrender my life to Christ. I renounce the Capitalist system."[13] Certainly years of preaching a social good works message had prepared numbers of American Protestants to approve of Roosevelt's actions.

But the New Deal did not elevate activist Protestants to national moral leadership. The heirs of the Progressives looked for supporters of progress in other places. The apostles of the Social Gospel had been moved by the shame of the cities; most city dwellers, however, did not belong to their congregations. The Archbishop of New York that Tammany Hall, or Franklin Roosevelt, had to be concerned with was the one in St. Patrick's, not the Bishop at St. John the Divine. Prohibition also played its part. The Northern wing of the Democratic party, which achieved repeal, was not disposed to think kindly of a class of people who had opposed it so solidly on the issue, however well-intentioned they might now be otherwise. The suspicion ran both ways. Walter Mondale's father, Theodore, a dirt-poor Methodist minister from rural Minnesota, voted for Norman Thomas in 1932, partly out of ideological sympathy, but also partly because FDR was a wet. In the parable, the laborers who began work in the morning were paid as much as those who joined up at the end of the day. Protestant social activists were paid nothing.

The postwar religion boom swept new members into Protestant churches of every stripe. But the activists had nothing to be active about until the civil rights movement. Here was a crusade made to order: a push to undo an old injustice, led by ministers. True, the ministers doing the leading were black. It is also true that the whites directly confronted by black self-assertion, who might conceivably have benefited most from pastoral counsel—Southerners and Northern city dwellers—also, for the most part, did not worship in liberal Protestant churches. Still, it was exhilarating. If they were not making history, the Protestant activists could at least feel that they were on its side. When the civil rights movement turned, rather suddenly, into a movement for black power—when ministers gave way to Maoists and Muslims—the white activists stayed with it. By then, of course, other causes began coming over the horizon: the Vietnam War followed, in quick succession, by women's and gay liberation. The churches, which had once told J. P. Morgan whom he must meet in his study, aspired to become the chaplain corps of the counterculture.

During all the twists and turns of the cutting edge, there were millions of white Protestants who had no sympathy with the most advanced forms of activism (70 percent of Protestant clergymen voted for Hoover in 1932). Other millions consciously resisted it, and modernist Biblical scholarship as well.

The great debacle of the resisters, celebrated in liberal folklore, had come with the Scopes trial in 1924, when the Mosaic science of William Jennings Bryan was held up to ridicule. The intellectual naïveté of Protestants served him ill in this instance. Clarence Darrow's devastating cross-examination of Bryan was, as Richard Weaver has pointed out,[14] a masterly diversion, for the point at issue in the trial in Dayton, Tennessee, was not science, Mosaic or modern, but the state's right to regulate the teaching of doctrines it deemed socially harmful. Bryan, hot to fight and win on every front, rushed eagerly into the trap.

But Dayton was only one battle in a decades-long series of retreats and withdrawals. *The Fundamentals: A Testimony to the Truth,* a series of pamphlets that gave Fundamentalism its name, was already by the 1910s a rear-guard action. Perhaps the most serious conservative loss came in 1929, when the Princeton Theological Seminary, the bulwark of fundamentalism in the Presbyterian church, abandoned the doctrine.

The only decent thing for conservative Protestants to do in the wake of their reverses, at least in the view of their enemies, was to disappear—preferably into those backwaters from whence they came: "over the town creek," as Mencken put it, "where the road

makes off for the hills."[15] Certainly they disappeared from the view
of the enlightened for a season. Will Herberg's *Protestant-Catholic-
Jew*, a Michelin guide to fifties religion, called fundamentalists and
charismatics "'fringe' sects," "hardly affecting the total picture."[16]
By 1968 the Thomas Road Baptist church was ninth largest in
America, though it might as well have been on the moon, for all
anyone noted the fact.

The first sign of life in conservative Protestantism that the wide
world noticed was the appearance in the fifties of a new generation
of evangelists, the most famous of whom was (and is) Billy Graham.
It is interesting to read a mainline churchman's judgment of
Graham, published in *Life* in 1957. Reinhold Neibuhr had been
active in the best Protestant intellectual circles for thirty years.
Politically he had moved from socialism to the Vital Center, that
rendezvous point of anticommunist liberals for whom he acted as a
kind of chaplain. Theologically he belonged to a loose movement
known as neo-orthodoxy, essentially an attempt, from within their
own ranks, to remind activist Protestants that their good works had
to be based on *something*. Graham's was not the kind of orthodoxy
he had in mind, however. Neibuhr was polite in *Life*. But the
evangelist, wrote the thinker, scanted "life's many ambiguities . . .
particularly so in a nuclear [age] with its great moral perplexities"—
and so forth, and so on.[17] Niebuhr pulled rank. That old-time
religion was not good enough for the Vital Center.

The second wave of conservative activity—Falwell's—began
when conservative Protestants found political issues they cared
about. The issues clustered around the third great dividing force in
American Protestantism, its encounter with modern morality.

All sects, Tocqueville had explained, preach the same morality.
So it was, for eighty some years, with liberal and conservative
Protestants. However they might read the word of God, or whatever
they might think of the social order, their attitudes toward sex and
family issues were similar. "The moral-familial perspective of nineteenth century Protestantism," as sociologist James Davison
Hunter puts it, "remained intact."[18] But only inertia kept it so.
Mainline thinking and philosophizing had been pulling away from
even thinking about such matters for decades. Even neo-orthodoxy
was no help. Karl Barth, who had a mistress for years, included a
correspondingly soft-edged passage on adultery in his *Church Dog-
matics*.[19] So when social custom began to fissure and slide in the
sixties and seventies, the schism spread to these issues as well.

Roe v. *Wade* was the main factor in Falwell's turn to politics. It was then, he had said, that "I was convinced that government was going bad. And I realized that it was, in part, because we had absented ourselves from the process." Conservative Washington politicos led him back into the process. "The gentlemen of the New Right showed me how I could get up an activist group legally. They had it all figured out." Paul Weyrich, the New Right gentleman who first uttered the phrase moral majority in passing, wasn't sure he liked it: it might seem, he feared, too arrogant. Falwell liked it.[20]

Liberal Protestants did not like it at all. "We object," ran a typical mainline counterblast, "to the list of issues which the religious right has identified as the moral agenda facing our nation." Their own agenda read like this: "to work for peace and things that make for peace, to seek justice for the poor, and to care for the created order" (whence the ammonites).[21] The disagreement was not just a matter of emphasis. The two sides disputed substance as well. Surveys of Christian elites find that on a range of social issues, the gap between mainline and fundamentalist Protestants varies from slight but noticeable to immense.*

The third wave of conservative activity was a run for the White House. In 1980 Falwell and other conservative evangelical ministers held a meeting in Dallas to plot electoral strategy. Pat Robertson, a charismatic Southern Baptist who had begun the Christian Broadcasting Network in 1960, excused himself, saying he had "no leading from the Lord" to participate in politics. Eight years later he was beating George Bush in the Iowa caucuses.

Robertson, though he was the son of a Virginia senator, had no political experience of his own. So slender were his qualifications that his campaign bio included among them the fact that he was a relative of William Henry Harrison. But he did have a constituency. At its mid-eighties heyday, CBN was anywhere from the second to the fifth largest cable television network in America, depending on who was counting. It took in more than $200 million a year in donations, used more WATS lines than the airlines, and had bureaus in London, Jerusalem, and Beirut. I asked Robertson, early on in his campaign, in his Virginia Beach headquarters, What does the religious right want? To put its issues on the agenda, he answered carefully. Then, carelessly: "We're like the thousand-pound gorilla. He sits where he wants to."[23]

---

*E.g., "Extramarital sex is wrong": mainline, 83%; fundamentalists, 91%. "Woman has right to abortion": mainline, 67%; fundamentalists, 17%.[22]

Not quite where he wants to, as it turned out. Robertson's campaign was clumsy, and his political ceiling proved to be rather low; once he had rebounded from his Iowa humiliation, George Bush ran better among Southern evangelicals than Robertson did. Falwell, as we have seen, has folded the Moral Majority up. When Jimmy Swaggart and Jim Bakker turned out to be as randy as Karl Barth, hostile observers predicted (hoped) that the the crusading evangelists might disappear altogether, though conservative Protestant uproar over two artistic images of Christ—*The Last Temptation of* and "Piss"—show that culture provides enough affronts to their sensibilities to keep them active. Garry Wills has even identified a fourth wave, after Graham, Falwell, and Robertson: the anti-abortion sit-in campaign Operation Rescue, whose leadership has passed from its Catholic founder to the charismatic Randall Terry.

Conservative Protestant strength should not be overrated. They have recovered nicely from Dayton, but they are not a majority, moral or otherwise. Though the Southern Baptists, the largest conservative denomination, are also the largest church in Protestantism—they overtook the United Methodists in the late sixties—the moderate denominations, in Roof and McKinney's typology, are together half again as large as the conservative ones. The liberal Protestant denominations come in fourth, a nose behind black Protestants. Conservative Protestantism's real strength is in the trend lines. Its vital statistics are better: Members of conservative denominations have larger families, and they tend to be younger. To an extent, this has long been the case. The moderate and liberal denominations used to make up for sluggish reproduction by what sociologists, with the cheerful rudeness of honesty, called "upward switching." The son of a hard-shell Baptist assembly line worker becomes Methodist when he lands his first white-collar job, Presbyterian when he receives his first promotion, and Episcopalian when he retires from the board of directors. The process still works, though less well. "Liberal and moderate mainline Protestants attract persons who are less active than those they lose to other groups, whereas those who switch to the conservative Protestant family are more active than those who leave."[24] Barring some unanticipated religious revival, and given the likely death rates due to their older memberships, the liberal churches are going to get a lot smaller before they ever get larger. These are the numbers that count, even more than the flashier statistics showing that there are fewer Presbyterians in America than Moslems, or fewer Episcopalians than there are Anglicans in Uganda. George Bush is the eleventh Episcopalian president of the United States. Will he be the last?

Time now for the theological question, So what? What do the ups and downs of Protestants matter to the millions of Americans who are Catholics, Jews, Mormons, Moslems, Rastafarians, humanists, or followers of Seth?

Non-Protestant believers are immediately affected by the fact that all established religions in America become Protiform. They Americanize themselves, which means they Protestantize themselves. Sometimes the process goes rather far. At the end of the nineteenth century, patriotic Irish Catholics were assimilating so enthusiastically that they drew a rebuke from the Vatican. Reformed Jews experimented with such innovations as Sunday services and organ music. Within Protestantism, the German-based Lutheran Church experienced an Americanizing movement of its own, whose partisans sought to change the Eucharist into a simple WASPy communion service. Each of these extreme manifestations was reined in, but every church and religion in this country that lasts undergoes, if it does not remain a cult, a more important external transformation: It becomes a denomination. It experiences, in Cuddihy's words, "what happens to [all] European religious and political beliefs when they land on American shores. They are civilized. They are taught to behave. They are tamed."[25]

Could a new teacher and tamer emerge? The Catholic Church is the obvious candidate. It has been the largest denomination in this country since 1850. Since World War II its members have been mounting the economic and status ladders by leaps and bounds. In the opinion of one scholar, the GI bill and the educational opportunity it gave young Catholic men "may have had more of an impact on the Catholic Church than the Second Vatican Council."[26]

But the more you look at the coming Catholic moment, the less meets the eye. The image that the hierarchy presents to the world is an unstable compound of traditional doctrines plus bits of modern theology picked up secondhand and old-hat from Protestantism. The laity has assimilated almost indistinguishably, which is a good thing, except that much of it seems to have assimilated to liberal Protestant norms: "The major denominational division" in Middletown, that philosopher's stone of sociologists, "is no longer the traditional Catholic–Protestant dichotomy" but the division "between the 'southern' Protestants and the more affluent and better-educated 'northern' Protestants and Catholics."[27] As an institution, the Catholic Church is lazy and fat. It is even losing its grip on the immigrant group that should have been a demographic windfall, the Hispanics, one-fifth of whom are now Protestant. Catholics are nowhere near a majority. Although the percentage of Americans expressing a religious preference for Protestantism sank by ten points from 1952 to 1985, it was still, at 57 percent, twice the number of those picking Catholicism.

Religions of all kinds remain a strong force in American life. "The hypothesis that modernization leads inevitably to secularization," wrote Theodore Caplow and his colleagues, "would be moderately plausible were it not for the American case." They go on to cite a cross-national study showing the "near disappearance of religious practice" among eighteen- to twenty-four-year-olds in half a dozen modern societies—but not this one. "The proportion of young adults . . . who think that religion should be very important in life ranges from 7 percent in France to 11 percent in Sweden, compared to 41 percent in the United States." "The proposition suggests itself," writes Walter Dean Burnham, "that the higher the level of development in a given society . . . the smaller will be the fraction of its population for whom religious beliefs are of great importance." But "the United States does not fit the main sequence at all."[28]

America is a religious nation. Protestantism is the religion of America. But it is now two religions, which means, practically, that it's none. The strength of American Protestantism had been its coherence—its expression, despite lively interdenominational warfare, of a unified view of the world, the way of the WASP at prayer. As such, it was a personal and cultural engine of enormous importance. For a hundred years, give or take, the engine has been knocking. It's getting worse, and repair is not in sight.

9

★

Three Places in the
Middle Atlantic States

WHEN WASPs first came here, they came first to the East Coast. There you find their oldest relics and maturest fruits. In New England and the South they developed two vivid subforms, similar enough to belong to the same civilization, different enough to tear it apart once. But New England and the South don't need redescribing. Beacon Hill and Mount Vernon get enough visitors; so for that matter do Stowe and Graceland. To get a sense of place, of WASPs in place, I picked three spots in between—two in the Hudson Valley and one on the Jersey shore.[1]

The town of New Paltz sits on a hill beside a small river, the Wallkill, a few miles west of the Hudson, and an hour and a half north of New York. The main street—a bus depot, pizza places—is Generic College Town. But before it crosses the Wallkill to the farms on the other side, a road called Huguenot Street turns off it to the right. The side street starts inauspiciously, with a burnt-out motel site and some condominiums. Then suddenly it turns into the late seventeenth century.

Huguenot Street bills itself, on the leaflets of the Huguenot Historical Society of New Paltz, as "the oldest street in America with its original houses." There are five of these, plus a small fort and a graveyard containing a reconstruction of the first stone church; the modern church on the street dates from 1839.

The Huguenots—originally a hostile nickname for French Calvinists, which, like Tory or Methodist, became simply a name—were one of Louis XIV's gifts to colonial America. Throughout the Sun

115

King's reign, they scattered over Protestant Europe. Some settled in the Rhineland principality of the Palatinate, which was called *Pfalz* in German. In the 1660s and 1670s some of these moved to New York. In 1677 twelve families got a grant of land and named their settlement New Paltz.

Their surnames—Bevier, Crispell, Deyo, DuBois, Freer, Hasbrouck, LeFevre—fill the graveyard. Some of them are still in the New Paltz phone book. There were also landless Huguenots in the settlement, as well as Dutch. But the intermarried grantees ran local affairs through a council called the *Duzine,* or dozen, an elected oligarchy, which was also hereditary: Membership in the Duzine was decided by vote of property owners, but the original families supplied all the candidates.

By the Revolution the percentage of Americans who were descendants of Huguenots was nearly the same as the percentage who are Jews today. If number crunchers had been available to make economic studies, the Huguenots would undoubtedly have fallen in the same place on their scales that Jews do—off them. They were, as a rule, skilled and prosperous. Louis Bevier, one of the first Duzine, left an estate of $90,000.

The historic stretch of Huguenot Street, about the length of two city blocks, is neatly self-contained. A crook in the road hides the condos. The town grew up the hill, away from the river. The oldest houses, all built before 1712, have stone walls, steeply pitched roofs, and thick Flemish chimneys. They look solid, well-grounded, slightly hobbity. One got a gingerbread wooden superstructure in the late nineteenth century, complete with a drive-through carriage porch. But the ground floor is still stone. The rest were never transformed. The fort, Fort Dubois, is also stone, built to withstand Indian raids; there are loopholes for rifles in the roadside wall. It was never attacked, and it is now a restaurant, the kind that fills up with tidy people for Sunday dinners. The most interesting building is the reconstructed church, which was rebuilt in 1972. It sits back from the street, behind a small patch of gravestones, and is a blend of "all mod cons" and authenticity. There are electric light in the sconces and a humidity-controlled manuscript room in the basement. The new/old cupola was lowered in place by helicopter. But the old design was followed as carefully as it could be recreated. The stones came from old walls in local fields; the communion table is period. The nineteenth-century church up the street has the neoclassical look, a temple with a steeple, of the typical old or pseudo-old American church (even when, as at Lynchburg, there are two sets of columns split-level). This building is small and square as a big toy—a candy box or a child's bank. The one original item is the seventeenth-century French Bible, which Jean Tebenin, a schoolmaster—not of one of the first families—willed to the church in 1730, directing that when French should no longer be spoken in services, it was to be auctioned, and the proceeds given to the poor. Now it is back in the pulpit.

The Huguenot imprint remained on New Paltz for some time. French remained the language of the local Reformed church until the middle of the eighteenth century, when it was replaced by Dutch. English didn't come in until 1800. In New Paltz, WASPs were parvenus, and second-wave parvenus at that. The Duzine stayed in business until the 1820s. But more remarkable is how completely Huguenots, there and elsewhere, disappeared, dissolving into generalized WASPiness. Huguenots, writes one of their historians, "had the instinct to blend." John Jay was a descendant of Huguenots, but he brought no French perspective to the Federalist Papers he managed to write. He was a supporter, in New York politics, of loyalty oaths for Catholics, which may have had something to do with an inherited opinion of the St. Bartholomew's Day Massacre. If so, he was not blended enough.

Prosperity, that great solvent, undoubtedly helped Huguenots fit in. So did their Calvinism. For whatever reasons, they vanished. *We The People,* an ethnic atlas based on the 1980 census, which pinpoints grouplets as tiny as Old Believers in Oregon and Gujarati Indians in the motel business, does not even mention them: "French," to experts in ethnicity today, means French Canadian or Cajun. They are the earliest example of assimilation, people who took up the customs of the country before there was a country. They had better things to do than stand apart. All they left in New Paltz is some surnames and a leafy street with two churches.

Across the river, a mile or two to the west, atop a sizable hill, is a small lake with a large resort hotel beside it. Mohonk Mountain House, like Huguenot Street, has a New Paltz address, but it is a different place, for it typifies a different time.

In 1869 a Quaker farmer living in Poughkeepsie with the uninventable name of Alfred Smiley visited Lake Mohonk for the first time. There was already a tavern on the spot. "When people got drunk and hard to manage," the owner "used to chain them to trees." But Smiley was struck by the setting—so much so that he persuaded his twin brother, Albert, a schoolteacher in Rhode Island, to join him in buying the entire mountain. They opened their own establishment the next year.

The Smileys never had to chain anyone to a tree, for they ran a dry house. That did not discourage guests. Schuyler Colfax, vice president of the United States, came during their third year in business. As business grew, so did the building. By 1910 there were several hundred rooms in an agglomeration of wings of wood and stone, surmounted by an array of turrets and cupolas. Abstractly considered, it was rather monstrous, in the grand Victorian manner, but it was done with complete conviction.

The great charm of the spot, however, was nature. The lake is snug and tapering, a quarter-hour canoe trip from end to end, with pine and stone cliffs on either side. Around the lake, up the cliffs, and across the outer slopes of the mountain winds a network of trails, well supplied with gazebos—round wooden seats under conical tops. Some of these look over Hudson River School panoramas, with hawks riding convenient air-columns; others direct the attention to jacks-in-the-pulpit. These are not confrontations with the antihuman nature that sometimes appears in Thoreau, or even immersions in Emerson's World-as-I. They offer a nature wonderfully balanced between wildness and accessibility. Nature to be looked at.

Inside the main house, guests could look at a decor that never quite gives way to belle epoque opulence. The most elaborate room, the Parlor, has its red velvet and chinoiseries, but there is enough open space under its high ceiling to prevent it from being as suffocating as the parlors of the people who first vacationed there.

Guests did not come there, however, just to relax, or even to edify themselves by studying vistas and efts. They also came to work. In 1879 Albert Smiley was appointed by President Hayes to the Board of Indian Commissioners. Four years later Mohonk hosted a Conference of Friends of the Indian, an annual event that continued until 1916. In 1895 the resort also held its first annual Conference on International Arbitration. One generous historian credits the get-togethers with supplying the "prototype of the modern foreign policy 'think-tank.'" Not the modern think tank, whose social configuration, as we have seen, is quite different. But the Mohonk conferences did assemble a good chunk of the WASP foreign policy establishment of the day, with honored foreign guests (Baron Takahira, Lord Bryce). It was the WASP establishment in the country.

Pictures show the Parlor filled with rows of beards, starched shirt fronts, wing collars. In 1912 Elihu Root and John Foster, Dulles's grandfather, both of them regular conferees, nominated Albert Smiley for the Nobel Peace Prize; he died before the committee could consider his nomination. Two years later the guns went off. Two years after that, Mohonk held its last conference.

The resort is still owned by the Smiley family, and it does a land-office business. There is cross-country skiing in the winter and tennis in the summer. There are murder-mystery weekends, bird-watching weekends, yoga weekends, meteor-shower weekends. There are numerous talks and lectures, many of them serious. There is still no bar, though one can order wine at dinner from a steward. Outside, there are still the lake and hills, the stars and the trout. But that sense of earnest and confident men and women, mingling public good and personal refreshment, lingers only in the mementos: in the Parlor, a grandfather clock, still ticking, presented to Mr. and Mrs. Albert Smiley at the tenth arbitration conference; next to it, the bust of an Indian; and in the hallway to the dining room, among the photographs of fawns and wildflowers, a gallery of faces of former guests, presidents hanging without precedence among clergymen. The type seems as long gone as the individuals. You would be as astonished to meet such a person as to run into Rutherford B. Hayes.

Ocean Grove, an entire town on the Jersey shore, is another resort. Like Mohonk, it once hosted presidents and also like Mohonk, it hosts them no longer. But as far as Ocean Grove is concerned, that has to be the presidents' fault, for it claims, with some truth, to be essentially what it was a century ago.

Though it is now far gone in seediness, the New Jersey coast was once the vacation spot of the rich of New York and Philadelphia. When the WASP upper classes began their infatuation with Anglo-Saxon exclusiveness, NO JEWS and KOSHER signs chased each other up and down the shore. The hotel wars passed over Ocean Grove, which was never intended for gentry and which had been explicitly founded as a Methodist community.

The town began as a camp meeting, a setting for revivalism and preaching. The first meeting was held the year Alfred Smiley discovered Mohonk. By 1872 the town had three hundred cottages and an open-air auditorium that seated ten thousand. It was dry; Sunday fishing, swimming, and sunbathing were also banned. Jew-

ish kids in Bradley Beach, the next town south, called it Ocean
Grave.

Ocean Grove was less obviously concerned than Mohonk with
changing the world. The emphasis was squarely on salvation. The
first president of the Camp Meeting Association described a meeting thus: "The people gather in warlike array, phalanx after phalanx: the helmet of salvation gleams, the breast plate of righteous-
ness [is] adjusted, the shield of faith wielded, the sword of the Spirit
girded, the feet shod with the preparation of the gospel of peace.
The divine commander cries, 'Fight the good fight of faith.'" But as
the imagery suggests, personal salvation was supposed to have
worldly effects, and world-changers came to claim their share of all
this energy. Ulysses Grant's mother and sister had a cottage nearby,
and he made his last public appearance at the Grove. James Gar-
field visited before he ran for president. The first candidate of the
Prohibition party was one of the founding members of the association. McKinley, Theodore Roosevelt, and Taft came as presidents;
Wilson and William Jennings Bryan as hopefuls. The town also
drew intellectuals and artists of various kinds. W. E. B. DuBois
spoke there. Heifitz and Kreisler played; Caruso sang (as did Margaret Wilson, Woodrow's daughter). In 1926 Sousa performed a
march, "The Wets and the Drys"; the implication of parity was so
disturbing that he wasn't asked back. Stephen Crane, of all people,
was taken there as a child. As a newspaperman, he wrote of
"sombre-hued" preachers "with black valises in their hands, and
rebukes to frivolity in their eyes. They greet each other with quiet
enthusiasm and immediately set about holding meetings."

A contemporary local historian of the place compares it, surprisingly at first glance, to the utopian communities of the early
nineteenth century: Brook Farm and the Fourierist phalanxes.
Like them, Ocean Grove "was at first experimental and always anti-
materialistic; and like them, it too evoked its share of cynical commentary." He goes on to note, with pardonable pride, that *his*
community has "outlived [the others] by far." The reason is that a
place like Ocean Grove had some relation to its social context.
There always were a lot more Methodists in America than Utopian
Socialists. Politicians and intellectuals look for other ways to reach
them, if they still try to reach them; the last president to go to Ocean
Grove was Nixon.

The two times I have been to Ocean Grove, once by train, once in
a car, I have come through Asbury Park, the slummy, run-down

town to the north. This is certainly the wrong way to come, though I wonder if there is a right way. There are numerous businesses in Ocean Grove—hotels, restaurants, an ice cream parlor—with no religious import, but the center of the place is still the Auditorium. The present structure, which is enclosed, was built in 1884. It is a hulking octagonal building, beige with chocolate trim. The electric cross on top can be seen for miles at sea. It is bounded on three sides by a permanent tent colony—platforms boarded up in the winter, which sprout white flaps in season. There is also a tiny park, in one of whose pavilions, the guidebooks inform you, there used to stand a miniature model of Jerusalem. The unkind Jersey weather eventually wore it away. To the north, across a narrow inlet, you can see the buildings of Asbury Park. One is topped with a looming sign, LIQUORS. Temptation.

Most of the buildings in town are two- to four-story wood frame houses and hotels. From a distance they look as if they might be charming. Up close they show themselves to be grossly overbuilt, squatting on their plots like fat men in phone booths. The economics of a seaside resort and the smallness of the original lots are probably responsible. The guests seem lopsidedly old, which must be the work of selection: A nonparty town will draw people who don't want to party. Many of the street names are religious— Pilgrim Pathway, Mt. Tabor Way. There is a Heck Avenue, undoubtedly named for a Mr. Heck, though it is hard not to think of it as a euphemism. The main drag runs down to a boardwalk and a narrow beach, where there are gulls and—the Northeastern touch—pigeons.

The larger currents have left Ocean Grove aside, but its own particular currents are still flowing. Bulletin boards on the boardwalks and in front of the Auditorium advertise concerts—the Ink Spots, barbershop championships—and of course dozens of sermons, Bible workshops, and gospel concerts. They start before Memorial Day and run past Labor Day. The musical ministry alone has more than forty programs.

Both times I was there, I found myself disliking the place with a fervor which seemed entirely out of proportion. The second time there I realized why—the tents.

These tents are not easy to get. They rent for as much as $2,000 a season, and there is a five-year waiting list for vacancies. Some people have occupied the same tent for thirty, even sixty years. Each tent has a sink, refrigerator, stove, and small bathroom. They are decorated according to the occupant's taste, some rather elaborately—flower boxes, samplers, striped awnings, hanging Japanese fish kites. They are no more than 4 feet apart, massed like cars in a parking lot.

As I walked along an alleyway that ran, between a real house and the tent colony, away from the Auditorium in the direction of Asbury Park, someone quite close behind me spoke. When I turned there was no one there. The remark had floated from one of the tents. It wasn't even clear from which.

There is no privacy. That koan-like tension between freedom and conformity that Tocqueville noted—everyone may practice his morality, for all morality will turn out to be the same—has here been shoved as far as it goes to the side of conformity. The *New York Times,* in a friendly summertime feature on the tenters, quoted one as saying, "she could stand in her tent and say, 'Heavens, I forgot my potato masher,' and hands would reach through the flaps, holding potato mashers." "You can't be enemies; you live too close," said another. "And you don't say anything in the tent you don't want published in the newspaper." "You want to argue," added a third, "you go out in the car."

As you drive away, the billboard that welcomed you as you came in bids you farewell: GOD BE WITH YOU TILL WE MEET AGAIN.

10
✳

The Post-WASP World, and How We Got Here

*T*HIS INVESTIGATION began with a symbol, George Bush. Let us consider another: the fact that in New York and no doubt in other large cities as well, it is possible, at least once a week when the weather is warm, to see someone, almost always a man, and by no means always a homeless man—his jeans or chinos are often clean, his track shoes new—pissing on the sidewalk.

The very triviality of the action makes it useful as an emblem of the fact that we are now in a post-WASP world. Illegitimacy, illiteracy, the homeless, the underclass, divorce, abortion, AIDS, crack, low productivity, sagging savings, better German cars, cheaper Japanese chips, the budget deficit—any of these issues to which the erosion of the national personality type might be relevant are so overdetermined, so explained and explained away, so subject to partisan pulling and hauling that it is hardly possible to give them a fresh look. The casual decision to relieve one's self here and now, and not later and elsewhere, is another matter. Since it is beyond public discussion, maybe we can talk about it.

Americans, WASP and non-WASP, have a long history of filthy roads. The material conditions of life in the days when there was little plumbing and few streets made it impossible for it to be otherwise. Philadelphia didn't have paved or swept streets until Benjamin Franklin turned his attention to the problem. "Some may think these trifling matters not worth minding or relating," Franklin notes, after devoting four pages of his *Autobiography* to his street improvement schemes in Philadelphia and London, but "human felicity is produced not so much by great pieces of good fortune that seldom happen as by little advantages that occur every day."[1] But now we have countless little advantages. On the scale of unpleasant actions, public urinating is pretty close to the minimum of offensiveness, a few cuts above littering. But that also means that, like littering, it is easy to avoid. When the streets are lined with shops, restaurants, and bars that, despite their PATRONS ONLY signs, are almost always open to anyone presentable, and sometimes open to anyone, what is the need? Would a working world of WASPs, literal and facsimile, have such slight reservoirs of patience and self-control? If the WASP world is not working, how did WASPs come to let themselves, and us, down? What does pissing in the street have to do with George Bush?

Chapter 3 presented an account of the elements of the WASP character, which because of historical circumstance became the American character. Chapters 6 through 8 looked at this character working itself out in various walks of life—and, nowadays, running out of energy, though in the arts the inhibitions it instilled remain robust. America is a tolerant country, and many things are tolerated here, even the American character. There are millions of Americans who behave as if the way of the WASP were still universally in force, millions more who behave as if they wished it were. But if we take a stroll around the pattern these days, we are likely to find it looking more and more like this.

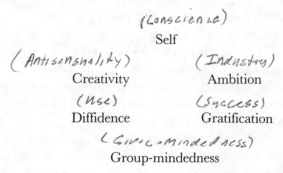

(Conscience)
Self

(Antisensuality)   (Industry)
Creativity   Ambition

(Use)   (Success)
Diffidence   Gratification

(Civic-mindedness)
Group-mindedness

The culture wars of Wall Street displayed an important shift, from the denial to the avowal of ambition. Ambition conscripts industry to the service of success. But in an ideal WASP world, no one should know that that is what's going on. Certainly no one should admit it, without numerous qualifications. ("We rightly desire honor and distinction. . . . But always we must remember, the glory is not ours.") Being too open about ambition devalues work as a good in itself. If success is a goal we avow, and not simply a condition we honor, and if less work—or shady work, or criminal work—leads there as well as hard work, why not take those paths?

Plenty of people disdained all the go-getters of eighties Wall Street, even the great majority of them who were not criminals. But money-making is not the only form post-WASP ambition takes. Intellectuals and subintellectuals—writers, academics, journalists—nourish their own desires, as insatiable as any of Ivan Boesky's, and as openly proclaimed. Norman Mailer is not the only writer to have done advertisements for himself, and Henry Kissinger is not the only scholar to have discovered the aphrodisiac of power. Sensitive souls who disdain the desire for pink Rolls-Royces lust for a Hollywood deal, an office in the West Wing, or a table at Elaine's and all the rewards appertaining thereto. The intelligentsia in fact reap the rewards of their ambitions far more cheaply than billionaires. Donald Trump would have to spend megabucks for the freedom to leave his wife. A poet gets to do that just for reading at a college.

With a shift in the motivations for work comes a shift in the nature of the goal, from success to gratification. Success is *defined* as gratification, which must be quick, if not instant. Logan Pearsall Smith accurately described the behavioral ideal of his class in late-nineteenth-century Philadelphia—spending all the hours of sunlight in great business buildings. Smith found the ideal "grotesque," and he fled it only by moving to Europe in 1888 (as millions of Italians and Jews and Poles, eager for a chance to live grotesquely, were streaming the other way). Today he could have saved himself the passage money.

The pursuit of gratification has its most dramatic effects not on the upper classes, but on the lowest. A middle-class teenage girl may well find the resources to help her deal with an unplanned pregnancy. Poor teenage mothers can only become wards of the state. Wall Street sometimes gives medical leave to bright young traders who stray into crack. There is no medical leave in East New York. The very poor are as different from you and me as the very rich, but the reason is not, as Hemingway might have said, that they have less money. The very poor, besides having less money, lead chaotic, unstructured, and therefore hopeless lives, which guarantee that they will always have less money. The main temptation to this kind of chaos is gratification.

On the face of it, there is still a lot of civic-mindedness in post-WASP society. Americans in politics are as eager as they ever were to avoid being stuck with the label "interests," as in *tools of special.* Are they eager to avoid behaving like them? It is true that, even in the days when we think of our institutions as working well, numerous Americans—slaveowners seeking the return of escaped property, manufacturers seeking protective tariffs—looked to the state to further their enterprises. Maybe what has changed most dramatically is the justifications we now offer for our actions, which in turn mold our actions. We are less likely to say that a program that benefits ourselves thereby benefits everyone. Benefiting ourselves is enough. America, Jesse Jackson says forthrightly, is a quilt made up of many patches: "the white, the Hispanic, the black, the Arab, the Jew, the woman, the native American, the small farmer, the business person, the environmentalist, the peace activist, the young, the old, the lesbian, the gay, and the disabled make up the American quilt."[2] But before the Rainbow Coalition, there was the Roosevelt Coalition: one week something for Southern whites, the next week something for Northern blacks; something for (tractable) businesses, followed by something for unions. On the other side of the aisle, the pollsters who saw an emerging Republican majority at the end of the sixties added up the groups and subgroups to whom they hoped to appeal—Catholic Germans in Wisconsin going hither, lower-class whites in East Texas going thither—like so many vegetables at a roadside stand. To these subcivic units—communities of class or ethnicity—must be added communities of cause. When Henry James, in *The Bostonians,* introduced Miss Birdseye, the nineteenth-century cause collector ("she belonged to the Short-Skirts league, as a matter of course; for she belonged to any and every league that had been founded for almost any purpose whatever"),[3] he was depicting a freak, an offshoot of Concord without genius, a deviation from deviants. Now Miss Birdseye is a force to be reckoned with in both parties. The prominence of both kinds of groups—the minority phalanxes which have seceded from America more effectively than the confederacy ever did, the cause addicts ceaselessly turning from one thing to the next, like sick men tossing in bed—is an inevitable consequence of Progressivism. If the goal of statesmanship is to steer down the

Mississippi River of history, the next channel might be anywhere, and anyone who claims to have found it must be heeded.

The babble of groups, each more importunate than the last, coexists oddly with a quality that looks like tolerance but might better be called diffidence. Under the way of the WASP, everything you might encounter in the world, apart from a handful of facts or injunctions, most of them located on the pattern, was subject to the test of use: What was it good for? Was it good for you? In the post-WASP world, more and more things are accorded the privilege of self-justification. They are, therefore we defer to them. It may be true that George Bush, as his shrink cousin said, had "a history of deferring to somebody up the line." But the new style of deference is much more inclusive. Post-WASPs defer, most obviously, to other cultures, religions, and ways of doing things. Do blacks speak a distinctive form of English? Teach it. Do Mexicans speak Spanish? Teach that too. The key word here is *other.* The collective opinions or behavior of our own culture are viewed with indifference or resentment. Post-WASPs defer to the natural world. There is, of course, a long WASP tradition of conservation. But a century and a quarter ago it was eccentric to couple this with a positive dislike of humanity: to enjoy the deaths caused by a shipwreck, as Thoreau did, or to take pleasure in recording, as Thoreau also did, the cabins and houses that had fallen empty and uninhabited around Walden Pond. Once, we went to nature for our own refreshment. Increasingly, we fence it off because it is our peer. The cumulative effect of multiple acts of deference—to other standards, cultures, even species—is insecurity, uncertainty, sheepishness: diffidence.

self-loathing

An impulse before which we show a great deal of diffidence is artistic creativity. It is symbolic of the status of this activity that the noun hardly needs the identifying adjective. Literally speaking, creativity can be manifested anywhere, from a constitutional convention to an auto body shop. But in common usage the word has been imperialized by the aesthetic. Creativity, in turn, demands and receives universal homage. We may not actually create beauty any more easily, as John Updike's career suggests, than we did in the days when Washington Irving had to escape to the time of Rip Van Winkle. But we honor the effort. Since we are all creative, or might be with proper encouragement, in honoring it we honor ourselves.

The brawls that occasionally erupt over whether or not ugly and inconvenient sculptures should block public thoroughfares or records of perversions should hang in galleries are side issues. Even the general question of public policy that underlies them—Should the state subsidize art?—is a triviality. If all tax-funded art expenditures stopped tomorrow (they won't) the only questions that would arise would be administrative and logistical. A god of our culture would have to rearrange its temples somewhat. It would be a god still.

The greatest god of the post-WASP world—actually, the same god, since creativity is a form of self-expression—is the self. The shift from conscience to self is a subtle one, so subtle that when Emerson made it, hardly anyone noticed. The conscience resides in the self, and the self is its audience. Yet the conscience is not *of* the self; it guides it, examines it, hectors it—and stands apart from it. The way of the WASP pared the moral world down to two beings: the self and its ever-present monitor. Simplifying still further, post-WASPs dispense with the monitor. The primacy of the self helps explain the tropism of diffidence toward "other" cultures. Logically, any collective pattern of behavior impinges on the self. But since we are most familiar with the constraints of the patterns we grew up with, we illogically expect strange patterns to be less demanding. Hence, an ex-Congregationalist can shout *nam myoho renge kyo* on his knees a thousand times a day, and still consider himself liberated.

The post-WASP traits—ambition, gratification, cause-mindedness, diffidence, creativity, self—are by no means universal. America is a big country, containing both St. John the Divine and Thomas Road Baptist. This is so despite the omnipresence of the media. The media, it was once thought, would be a great homogenizing force in American life; certainly it has broken down regionalism. At the same time, however, it has turned out to be a heightener of differences among individuals, wherever they live. Falwell and Robertson, after all, rose to prominence on television. Everything is everywhere, which means that anyone may be anything.

Like a chick with shell on its back, the new traits still retain traces of the old. The puritanism of antisensuality often reappears, displaced onto health and fitness. Robin Byrd, who hosts a popular pornographic show on cable TV, on which she interviews strippers and blue movie stars, also does a second show on which she demonstrates weightlifting. No doubt she is a nonsmoker.

For years students of the culture have been trying to give the constellation of post-WASP traits a name. Tom Wolfe came up with

the "Me Decade," soon to become the "Me Quarter of a Century."
Christopher Lasch deplored the advent of narcissism. Charles
Reich hailed Consciousness III. They all do their subject too much
honor. The new traits do not constitute a type, nor have they
coalesced into a character. They have not passed through the
necessary formative historical experiences. The way of the WASP
had a prehistory in English politics and Reformation religion. It
took shape in the course of founding colonies, fighting a revolution,
and, most important, fashioning a state. The new dispositions that
crowd the national mind have not seen enough or done enough.
They are reactions, rebellions. They are as new as the elements
uranium passes through as it decays into lead, and about as stable.
They are enough to define a post-WASP world, not a post-WASP
character.

How did we get here? There are two common explanations of the
birth of the post-WASP world, one sociological, one intellectual.
Neither one does the job.

   The sociologically inclined link the rise of new habits—rather,
the debility of old ones—to the post–World War II rise of a new
class. This new class is called many things, most often simply the
"new class." Theodore White noticed it twenty years ago, "pumped
out into suburbia, at least in the East . . . by the education explosion
of the past fifteen years": "administrators, teachers, scientists, civil
servants, technicians, bureaucrats, corporate-enmeshed types."[4]
John Updike described them, in *Couples*, arriving in Tarbox, Massachusetts, in the late fifties, where they "tried to improvise . . . a
fresh way of life. Duty and work yielded as ideals to truth and fun.
Virtue was no longer to be sought in temple or marketplace but in
the home—one's own home, and then the homes of one's
friends"[5]—including the bedrooms.

   This class was more than a generational artifact. It came into
being before the Baby Boom—the couples in *Couples* were twenty to
twenty-five years too old for the boom, and only their children, by
first and second marriages, would belong to that endlessly dis-
cussed generation—and it continues to recruit new members after
the boom has subsided. The class's distinctiveness depends rather
on its experiences and its occupations. The decisive factor in both
was higher education. The new class had had it, and having it was
neither a social grace nor a professional apprenticeship, but a
necessary general background for handling the information their

jobs required them to digest. A strong dose of general knowledge, followed by a continuous lifetime infusion of it, the new class theory implies, is an inevitable solvent of traditional behavior.

But this cannot be a sufficient explanation. There have been plenty of educated Americans who felt no temptation to stray from the way of the WASP. Jonathan Edwards, who entered Yale at the age of thirteen, was as well-schooled as anyone there now. Benjamin Franklin was at least as intelligent as Joe Biden.

If higher education *per se* isn't to blame, then perhaps what the educated were taught is. This is the burden of the intellectual explanation. The moral and intellectual defenses of the WASP world, in this view, succumbed to a modernist intellectual blitzkrieg. Marx and Freud—and, in Allan Bloom's version, Nietzsche and Heidegger—commanded the assault. Mann and Kafka, and English-speaking auxiliaries like Eliot and Joyce, gave cultural support. The *Schwerpunkt,* the focus of the attack, was nothing less than conscience and industry: the way of the WASP in its private and economic manifestations. The inhabitants of the WASP world thought their inner lives were righteous and their social order just. Modernism showed the fresh-faced future members of the new class that the private life was plagued by neurosis and that society was founded on exploitation. WASPs, born or self-made, were as wholesome as the hollow men, as doomed as the Buddenbrooks family.

The intellectual theory does not hold that many, or even more than a handful of, postwar American educators, still less their students, were actual Marxists. Marx himself had a lifelong suspicion of "Yankee socialists," and American Marxist parties have always been politically trivial. Psychoanalysis has had a wider American vogue, though Freud was even more caustic about his American admirers. Conscripting Joyce or Eliot for such a project, finally, involves major distortions of what they were up to. The intellectual theory does hold, however, that American higher education became infused with a modernist mood, even as, in earlier times, it had been infused with religious or commercial moods, and that this mood, communicated to the postwar influx of college students, loosened their mooring to what we have called the WASP world. In the fifties the mood took the form of a conservative skepticism that lurked behind the end of ideology. In the sixties, radicalized, it took to the streets. In the eighties it gave us Allan Bloom's "nice" students, dulled by mental anomie.

Multiply modernism in higher education by all the alienating forces in nonacademic culture, high and low, somber and ludicrous, from *Partisan Review* to *Mad Magazine,* and you have an adequate explanation of what happened to the WASP world.

The intellectual explanation goes farther than the sociological explanation, and both are true as far as they go. But they do not go far enough.

But let us take an example.

In 1896 Columbia University dedicated its present site on Morningside Heights in Manhattan, a few blocks north of St. John the Divine. President Seth Low, future mayor of New York, called Columbia "a university . . . set on a hill." Abraham Hewitt, the current mayor, explained what it was set on a hill for: "against its walls the waves of communism and anarchy will . . . beat in vain."[6] Not in vain, at least not in the long run, for in 1968 anarchy took over the campus. In the late thirties, almost midway between the Low–Hewitt era and Mark Rudd, Lionel Trilling was dropped from the Columbia English department, then reappointed to it. His experience and his subsequent career bridge the two extremes.

Lionel Trilling's early difficulties and ultimate triumph at Columbia are part of the lore of New York intellectuals, a tale that has been told and retold. It is, in part, a tale of WASP discrimination—in this case, anti-Semitism. For in 1936 Trilling, a young Jewish English instructor struggling to finish his PhD dissertation, was informed by the department, a "bastion of Anglo-Saxon gentility,"[7] that he would not be reappointed, because "as . . . a Jew" he would be "more comfortable" elsewhere.

But Jewishness was not the only thing on Columbia's mind; there were already Jewish professors in other departments. The English department also told Trilling that his being "a Freudian [and] a Marxist"[8]—that is, a modernist—was making him uncomfortable on Morningside Heights. Trilling's attachment to these dogmas was neither lighthearted nor sentimental. In 1929 he had moved to Greenwich Village, still the capital of radical bohemia. "One must be close to one's land," he wrote in a book review in 1930, "passionately close in some way or other, and the only way to be close to America is to hate it."[9] He worked part-time briefly for a Communist front group and remained interested in revolutionary politics for some years even after becoming disillusioned with the Party.

Trilling, finally, had been in a mental slump, familiar to graduate students, slogging away at his dissertation for four unproductive years. The English department's notification galvanized him. He went to the professors he knew best and told them they were losing someone good. The department reversed itself. Three years later Trilling's dissertation was published, and he sent a copy to Nicholas Murray Butler, the president of the university, who invited the young instructor and his wife to dinner.

The dinner at the Butlers was a rich moment, worthy of the fiction Trilling would spend his career explicating. Butler had been president of Columbia for thirty-seven years. He had lost a bid for a Republican presidential nomination, won a Nobel Peace Prize. A dinner at Butler's was not like a dinner in the Village. "A terrible thought came to me," Diana Trilling recalled four decades afterward: "Need I wear long white gloves?" She called *Vogue*, which told her that no host required long white gloves any more, except the King of England. "This convinced me: long white gloves would be worn at President Butler's." After dinner Butler led the men, all faculty members, to his library for brandy and cigars, where he recounted an anecdote that had nothing to do with Trilling specifically, though the punchline was obvious enough. "At Columbia, sir, we recognize merit, not race."[10] A few months later Trilling was made an assistant professor.

What is most interesting for our purposes is not Trilling's victory but Columbia's decision. This was as complicated as the earlier decision to dump him had been. The English department and the university went out of their way to keep him, in part because he was right about himself. He was good, and once he told his superiors this fact and pulled his dissertation together, they were obliged to recognize it.

The radicalism that had given offense had also virtually worn away by the end of the thirties. Trilling found that he was more interested in culture than in politics—in struggles of perception and self-definition, not of classes. It had virtually worn away, but not quite. Trilling's focus may have shifted, by the quiet fifties, from the proletariat to Henry James's characters, but they too suffered from oppressions and impediments to authenticity—as did, implicitly, the students he taught. When, in the sixties, the discussions of authenticity took a noisier form, Trilling did not approve. "No one ever thought that when [modernist] writers represented violence as interesting or beneficent," he complained to a reporter in 1969, "they were really urging their readers to bloody actions."[11] He may not have thought such a thing, at least not for thirty years. But modernism in the streets, or on the steps of Low Library, was still a form of modernism.

When Columbia took Trilling back, it was also clearly feeling guilty about its own group-mindedness. For group-mindedness violates the way of the WASP, as any honest and intelligent WASP must eventually recognize. So Columbia righted the wrong it had done. But it did more: It opened itself to a modernist, to a Freudian and a Marxist, however mellowed. This is the long-term damage WASP group-mindedness does to the WASP world. In their guilt, WASPs not only do the right thing by those who wish to become WASPs, but they extend themselves for the benefit of those who intend to remain something else.

Finally, was Columbia simply tired? The "Anglo-Saxon bastion," writes a critic of Trilling, had been shaken "by two decades of assault on the genteel tradition and the social-economic system that underlay it."[12] That assault, in the twenties and the teens, had not been Trilling's modernism, but the railing of H. L. Mencken or, at a higher level, D. H. Lawrence. But why should that have shaken anybody? The way of the WASP had been quite capable of handling such assaults. As late as 1915, the trustees of the University of Pennsylvania kicked Scott Nearing, a socialist economics professor, off the faculty of the Wharton School (Mencken defended him). This was a brutal, hence ultimately counterproductive, move. But throughout the nineteenth century the WASP world had resisted strange ideas that were actually or potentially hostile by simple imperturbability. Seventy-five years of heavy Catholic immigration finally produced Al Smith, who wanted to know what the hell a papal encyclical was. Socialists raged and raved and never broke out of single digits on election day, beyond ethnic ghettos.

The fatal mood that came to pervade higher education was not, then, *mitteleuropaisch* modernism, at least not at first, but the WASPs' own loss of direction. This showed itself, as we have seen, in an infatuation with progressive politics and in religious confusion. It showed itself even in the Columbia English department. Maybe Freud and Marx were the next bend in the river of literary criticism, if not of history; and certainly no one on Morningside Heights was going to object to a Freudian/Marxist on the basis of that oldtime religion. WASPs could not tame modernism, as they had Catholicism, or exclude it, as they had European socialism, because, although they remembered when to wear long white gloves, they had forgotten what they themselves stood for. They ran for president and won Nobel Prizes, yet they were weak. Modernists lived in the Village (then a low-rent neighborhood) and wrote obscure essays about hating America, yet they were vital. Vital enough, anyway, to permeate higher education. Modernism was a secondary infection, and the new class was a secondary victim. The damage had already been done, by WASPs themselves, to their own world.

This is the historical responsibility of the WASP elite—the class of which George Bush is a late and personally unconfused, though inarticulate, member. They are how we got here.

The postwar new class was opened to new opinions not because it wore white collars or had earned sheepskins. It was exposed to solvent ideas because the people who should have repelled them, by force of example if not by actual force, had fallen down on the job. Although we have tried to keep the concept of an elite out of the argument as much as possible, because it has distorted the common meaning of the word WASP and because in a democratic society, the very function of an elite is elusive and indirect, here it gives us a foothold in the scree of facts. Even if the power of an elite is diluted by democratic politics and egalitarian custom; even if the leadership it exercises consists in the mere circumstance that it is at the head of the parade, though the music may be coming from elsewhere, the fact remains that an elite, if it exists, is at the head. Elites by definition have visibility; they are the people to whom attention must be paid. If only some (well-placed) WASPs were persuaded by progressive politics and liberal Protestantism, it was enough to disable the WASP elite as a class. This, for all their success, is the pathos of the Falwells and the Robertsons, of invisible bestsellers like *In His Steps,* of Grahams patronized by Niebuhrs. People outside the elite can form television networks, transform politics, run for president. So long as the elites exclude them, they still, in some sense, lack resonance. They are like a tree falling where no one who counts can hear.

Three years ago the scandal of the Marine guards at the Moscow Embassy threatened to provoke an interesting discussion of elite irresponsibility and cultural power. Two young Marines allowed themselves to be seduced by Soviet agents, whom they gave access to secrets in the embassy they were supposed to guard. Why had Marines, supposedly *semper fidelis,* proved faithless? The commander of the Corps speculated that it had to do with a breakdown of religion and morality back home. At which point Lars-Erik Nelson, an intelligent liberal columnist, did some digging and found that the guilty leathernecks were both from devout, conservative Protestant families. One was the son of a Pentecostalist minister. There hadn't been any breakdown in their lives.

Point to secularism? Not so fast. The Marines were responsible for their actions, but other people were also responsible for the security situation at the embassy. The ambassador, who had not disapproved of Marine fraternization with Soviet citizens or of a heavy Soviet presence of servants within the embassy, was a career Foreign Service officer, and hence most unlikely to be the son of a Pentecostalist minister. Was his laxness in any way attributable to his background? What punishments were the Marines—or outright spies, like the Walkers—given, *pour encourager les autres,* and how were these influenced by prevailing judicial norms? Can tongue-speakers be expected to mind the store all by themselves when Episcopalians go fishing?

Society is of a piece. Even if it is in pieces, they rub up against each other. Example is a great force for reinforcement, and everyone may be an example. It is possible for a group or an individual to buck the multitude; it is even possible for them to buck their leaders. In the case of elite dereliction, it may be necessary. But it isn't easy.

The George Bushes of the world bear more responsibility for the pissing in the street than they may be aware of.

11

★

Can the Way of
the WASP Be Saved?

*I*T IS TIME—maybe long past time—for some objections. We have been holding forth like Butler in his library, or Dr. Robertiello's fellow guests. Time for the critics—who are ourselves, too—to speak up.

All objections come under one grand objection. If the way of the WASP is so good, why is it in trouble? Why would people defect from something that was self-evidently superior? One of the qualities to be expected of a good social or moral order is durability. Aren't defections a sign that the way itself is flawed, that it is internally contradictory, or that it fails to satisfy, in any realistic fashion, unignorable human needs?

What odds would an actuary give for a view of the world that was as suspicious of sensuality as the WASP's is? Did WASPs err in making the casual pleasures of everyday life too lean? Industry requires the delay of gratification. Has it been delayed too long? The Chinese work hard; so do the Italians. Yet they both know how to cook. Is there some lesson here? Are chicken chow mein and spaghetti with meat balls a sufficient corrective (or even Hong Kong shrimp and tiramisu)? A culture can add new customs here and there, just as it can build opera houses and art museums. But if some basic impulse is still being frustrated, the only alternatives are change or disaffection.

The same kinds of frustrations swirl around creativity. Fun, on the one hand, and high seriousness, on the other (the arts are "good for you"), can buy a lot of time, but ultimately they are

137

evasions, as anyone with a creative urge senses. A country can consign the bulk of its music to drunks, drug addicts, blacks, and imported Europeans for only so long. The same with all the other arts. It isn't just that the content of so much art, good and bad, is subversive, though it is: Parents may object to heavy metal lyrics, but if their children study French in college, or even in advanced classes in high school, they will be assigned *Les Fleurs du Mal,* in which they can read about the head of the murdered mistress sitting on a table top "like a ranunculus." The forms of beauty—the concentration required to understand it, the effort needed to produce it—make their own demands as well. A poem, simply because it is a sonnet, is an ambassador from another world, whether it is about perversion or about sunsets. A rhyme scheme is as subversive in its way as a severed head.

A plausible case can be made that social censorship is good for art. Since most people have little or no talent, a general climate of contempt for creativity will discourage all but the truly driven. Philistinism drives the Joyces into exile, but at least only the Joyces will be writing. Such a cynical argument, however, is anathema to both the serious artist and the serious WASP.

Hungry nerve endings and unhappy artists are not the only sources of frustration the WASP world makes for itself. In a system where the premium placed on success is so high and in which, as in every system, not everyone will be successful, is the psychological burden of not succeeding too heavy? Did the way of the WASP make failure intolerable? A Hindu can always blame karma, a Moslem may shrug and say *inshallah.* Catholic Europeans don't think the score is kept in such worldly terms: The Austrian Catholic journalist Erik von Kuehnelt-Leddihn is fond of pointing out that the directors of the national banks of countries like Ireland and France are traditionally Protestants, with a sprinkling of Jews. But the WASP's favorite scripture is the parable of the talents, and he knows the lazy servant has no one to blame but himself. WASP's self-punishment makes them bad candidates for collective action, as socialists have long noted with disgust, and in that sense the disposition to take economic failure personally is socially stabilizing. But backed-up pools of bitterness remain: Love Canals of potential resentment. If a demagogue doesn't tap them, then a guru will: It wasn't your real self that failed, only a false one; the solution is to find your self. You find it, naturally, outside the way of the WASP.

There are other contradictions embedded in the economic injunctions of the way of the WASP. We have already noted the disruptive potential of ambition, whenever it suddenly rears up between industry and success. There is more. Modern students and critics of capitalism—Joseph Schumpeter, Daniel Bell—have worried about its self-destructiveness, the tendency of prosperity to undermine the morality that produces it. John Wesley wrote about the same process, though his main concern was for morality, not prosperity. Religion "must necessarily produce both industry and frugality, and these cannot but produce riches. But as riches increase, so will pride, anger, and love of the world in all its branches. How then is it possible that Methodism, that is a religion of the heart, though it flourishes now as the green bay tree, should continue in this state? For the Methodists in every place grow diligent and frugal; consequently they increase in goods. Hence, they proportionately increase in pride, in anger, in the desire of the flesh, the desire of the eyes, and the pride of life. . . . Is there no way to prevent this?"[1] If the cycle of attitudes, from industriousness to enjoyment to indulgence, were simply a matter of individuals—of families, rising from shabbiness and sinking back to shabby gentility in three or four generations—there might be no cause for cultural concern. New individuals and families would always be ready to start the cycle anew: for every Logan Pearsall Smith emigrating in first class, ten wannabe Smiths immigrating in steerage. But of course it doesn't work that way. People aren't hermetic; they communicate their new conclusions. Logan Smiths write books; John Smiths raise children. The influx of newcomers eager to begin the game may not be enough to balance the disaffection of old players.

Given their peculiar attitude toward thought, how can WASPs be expected to resist new conclusions over the long haul? It is not that WASPs are unable to think, exactly. In any heavenly symposium of political philosophers, Hamilton, Madison, Jefferson, and Lincoln will have seats at the head table. It's that WASPs seem to do their thinking in bursts—a lightning flash of brilliance, with decades of darkness until the next one. Their belief in the clearness of truth and the high priority they place on use both account for this. If the right thing is plain, what use are thinkers? When a historical crisis, generated by some hostile force or unnoticed contradiction, comes along, some individuals will rise to the task of thinking about it. But the very clarity of their efforts discourages revision. What sane man would set himself up to tinker with *The Federalist Papers* or with Lincoln's Second Inaugural?

The effect of these occasional exertions, however, is to encourage a general sluggishness. When challenging thoughts appear, the WASP is slow to defend himself. It is possible for a culture to think too much for its own good. If one had to choose between Warren Harding and the culture that produced him, and Heidegger and the culture that produced him—between the man whose associates cut taxes and the man whose associates killed Jews—one would obviously choose Harding. But if a culture doesn't think at all, how can it repel the hundreds of errors, Heideggerian and otherwise, that are abroad in the world? Mencken complained long and loud about the parochialism of the American mind, its addiction to European ideas that were both half-baked and stale. He himself was a gaudy instance of this parochialism, hawking, as hot off the presses, his watered-down Huxley and *Cliff Notes* Nietzsche in a style pitched to the level of college sophomores, which is about as high as WASPs ever feel the need to go, between Jeffersons. And Mencken was one of the best of his breed, because at least some of his aesthetic instincts were good. Beneath their armor of innocence, WASPs have the resistance of eighteenth-century Indians. If there is any smallpox in the air, their intellectuals will come down with it.

The final contradiction—perhaps it is a temptation—is embodied in the question, *Who cares?* Who cares about the world, even the world of the WASP? This is a question WASPs occasionally ask themselves, and whenever they do, it means conscience is straining away from civic-mindedness. For despite all their social concern, despite their devotion to labors that are generally beneficial, there is a querulous, Quakery, go-to-hell, we'll-go-it-alone state of mind which WASPs often find appealing. The most famous rejectionist communities in American life—the Old Order Amish, the Hutterites—have their roots in the German Reformation, but WASPs feel the tug too. It is endemic, if latent, in their kind of Protestantism. If you can't change the world, then let it go. There is another, which conscience glimpses from time to time. A glimpse may be enough. So, in a strange combination of pride and humility, the WASP retires. Pride from his sense of cultural proprietorship: It's our party, we can leave if we want to. Humility from a peculiar understanding of the Christian example he can find strangely seductive. "Mild He lays His glory by," wrote John Wesley's brother

Charles ("Hark! The Herald Angels Sing"). Why should the WASP's infinitely lesser glories fare any differently?

If the WASP world suffers from all these frustrations and tensions, gaps and allurements, could it ever have endured? If it can't last, why should we bother trying to restore it?

12

★

Can the Way of the WASP Save America?

WHAT, then, would be better? Since we are not talking about higher mathematics or ancient history, but about how we live, critics have an obligation to answer this question. If the way we once lived was wrong, what are the alternatives? And since the experience of every revolution since the French has shown that men can't simply make up societies, as if from a hotel laundry list or a Chinese take-out menu, what are the alternatives concretely available?

Who lives better? Let us approach this question with a minimum of diffidence, beginning with the life-styles of the self-created others—"alternative" life-styles. After twenty years there are still flower children. There is also, in a museum in Durban, South Africa, a dodo skeleton. The two are equally lively. Twenty years from now, the punks and skinheads of today will have joined the exhibits. Radical feminism is absurd—nine parts lesbianism, one part goddess worship. The male homosexual community has all it can do to stay alive. Twenty years ago there was a lot of talk, much of it sociologically respectable, about the uniqueness of the inner-city black family structure, about the persistence of matriarchy, perhaps from as far back as Africa. There is still talk about the inner-city black family structure today, although it now goes under the rubric "underclass." The new talk is unintentionally hostile and ultimately unhelpful. But so was all the approving talk of matriarchy.

Does the rest of the world live better? The Third World, for instance? The short answer is that if it did, it would be the First

World. But let us be a little more specific. China? Inventors of printing and gunpowder and all the art of East Asia, one civilization for three millennia—these are not small achievements. But that civilization is also subject to grotesque convulsions of unimaginable destructiveness. The current one has been going on since the Taiping rebellion. Its most dynamic agent murdered more people than Stalin and Hitler combined. India? The wounded civilization—the phrase is V. S. Naipaul's—obsessed with excrement, worshipers of Kali, which is to say, death? The Arab world? Yes, everyone who saw *Lawrence of Arabia* heard Alec Guinness say that medieval Cordoba had street lights. But when the bottom fell out, it fell pretty far. All the treasure of OPEC has been put to no better use than buying a few baubles, here an AWACS, there a desert soccer field, as economically productive as money in a mattress. Africa? Last stand of smallpox, and first stand of AIDS? Where the most prosperous blacks are the ones ruled by the Boers? Latin America? The wounded civilization across our border, where the conservatives are mercantilists, and the revolutionaries are Maryknoll nuns who have just discovered Karl Marx? The current Peronist president of Argentina, Carlos Menem, is the son of Syrian immigrants. What is the problem with his country—that sons of immigrants become presidents, or that they become Peronists?

What about the societies in our own economic league, to which we have more resemblances, material or cultural or both? You can't go through an airport bookstore without finding some admiring treatise on Japanese management methods, or through an airport lounge without spotting some briefcased would-be junior executive who is reading one. But, even if it were possible, do we seriously propose to imitate that tightly controlled and controlling culture, bound in deference and group-think? The Soviet Union, whose economy, if it does not succeed in becoming the West's largest welfare recipient, will break up even faster than its raj? Israel—that unstable coalition of imperialists and pacifists, theocrats and socialists? Central Europe? Where they have to build extra closets to hold their Nobel Prizes for literature, and where spring has finally, and thrillingly, come—about time, after eighty years of woe, almost all of it generated by the stupidity and incompetence of the central Europeans themselves? Sweden? The state as crib, with sex and alcohol as pacifiers? Italy? Which taught Europe the meaning of civil society two thousand years ago and then, perhaps from boredom, forgot the lesson itself? England, which has needed eleven years of the Iron Lady to break the back-scratching embrace of Labor socialists and Tory socialists, and which may not yet have broken it? France, our brothers in freedom who, after two empires, two monarchies, five republics, and fascism, seem finally to have gotten the hang of it?

This catalogue of vices and shortcomings has grown a bit rhetorical, but immigration figures are not rhetorical. The borders are open. Planes and boats leave this country every day. It is as easy to cross the Rio Grande going south as it is to cross it going north. If you push off from Key West in a dinghy, there is a fair chance you will reach Haiti. So why is it that the traffic is so overwhelmingly one way? Why do we have to employ a police force to patrol the borders and to raid sweat shops to pick up the wretches who evaded the border patrol's grasp? Why aren't Brooklyn Jews clamoring to go to Odessa, or Motor City Arabs begging to be settled in Beirut? If the society the WASPs built weren't safer, freer, and richer than any other—if it didn't offer less likelihood of being arrested for voting wrong or praying oddly, or more chance of accumulating a nest egg and keeping it—would so many people want to come here?

Many of these societies, to be fair, have the great mitigating advantage of history. Adam Smith said there is a lot of ruin in a nation. There is more of it—that is, more capacity to endure it—the longer there has been a nation. Wherever the past lies compost-thick, it provides some psychological security against crime and madness. Even under Hitler or Stalin, those who suffered might think: There will come a time when the incubi will be gone, and Germany and Russia will remain. America, a nation founded on a set of ideas and dispositions—the ones we have been discussing—has no such fallback.

Deciding that a way of life is preferable to the alternatives does not guarantee that it will survive or prevail. Putting a comparative value on the way of the WASP, however, makes it easier to judge the costs it imposes on those who follow it—costs of the kind outlined in the preceding chapter. If the benefits of WASP civilization outweigh any others we are likely to find, we can decide to feel its discontents less keenly.

There is another point of comparison, closer to home—the way we have increasingly come to live since the WASPs began losing their way. In fairness to all the WASPs who went astray, they had no experience to go on when they first did so, only hopes. Progressivism promised energetic government and national unity; liberal

Protestantism offered accurate scriptural scholarship and social uplift. If they had known they were exchanging the life they knew—even the problems they knew—not for these pleasant prospects but for ambition, gratification, cause-mindedness, diffidence, creativity (a stab at it, anyway), and self, they might well not have done it. Now they, and we, know. The results are in. We might be willing to contemplate a renaissance.

If George Bush, Episcopalian of Kennebunkport, and John Sununu, Lebanese Catholic born in Havana, decided to contemplate the politics of a renaissance—that is, to examine some of the problems that faced them and the country in the light of WASP values— what might those two WASPs come up with?

They would find justification for certain things that they want to do anyway. All his political life, George Bush has been interested in lowering taxes on capital gains, the profits made on selling investments. It was a specific proposal he could point to, virtually his only one, even in the darkest days of the vision thing. As a result of the tax reform package of the last years of the Reagan administration, the capital gains tax rate actually went up. The American capital gains tax rate is now high relative to the rates of other industrial countries, and higher than it has historically been relative to our own income tax rates. The raising of the capital gains tax rate was not an unmixed blunder: A whole industry of tax shelters designed to simulate capital gains dried up. But the pool of legitimate venture capital—money for new enterprises that banks might not be willing to bankroll—also shrunk. What do we want rich people to do with their money, buy paintings or "devote their lives to making more"? Industry and success would help Bush explain his own preference for the latter.

Bush has said that he wants to be an education president. Members of his party have argued that education would benefit from increased parental choice among school districts; Republican educational radicals even favor choice between public and private schools, facilitated by tuition tax credits or vouchers. The best defense of such plans is the test of use. In an era of cultural consensus, education policy might conceivably have been left to the direction of professionals and bureaucrats. In the absence of such a consensus, variety is the best way of allowing parents to see what different styles of education are good for. Word of good techniques will get around, as WASPs once used to assume it would, whether the techniques concerned colonial assemblies or assembly lines. A use-oriented public would at least be willing to give variety a try, since America's education monoliths have been turning out students who are increasingly good for nothing.

The Bush administration could even bring some order to federal art funding. The art world, or that part of it which depends on federal grants, has always suspected Republicans of being unenthusiastic patrons. They are, though they spend the money anyway, because creativity is a god and Republicans are nothing if not pious. Washington could say that, in a new WASP world, it will abandon the attempt to force creativity like bulbs in winter, and limit spending to the work of artists who are dead. Taxes would still help pay for Beethoven—even Ives, if anyone wanted to listen. Even Mapplethorpe, come to think of it (there is no perfect solution). Public television could devote itself entirely to what it already does best: broadcasting the classics of Hollywood, in which Orson Welles and Fred Astaire and John Wayne stumbled into greatness under the cover of entertainment.

But Bush and Sununu would also find that a WASP renaissance would impel them to do things they don't want to do or haven't been willing to risk.

Returning to a new WASP world would mean declaring war on group-mindedness in all its forms. Bush's instincts, and Republican instincts generally, are to buy off clamorous groups with an etiquette of tokenism. Not surprisingly, they often defer to the worst tokens. For his first year in office, Bush went out of his way to court Jesse Jackson, the most forthright ideologist of group-think in America today. During the last ten years, meanwhile, the most forthright opponent of group-mindedness in Washington was not a Republican at all, but Morris Abram, a liberal Democratic civil rights lawyer Ronald Reagan appointed to the Civil Rights Commission. Abram found himself in the curious position of being to the right of most of the Republican party because, having once adopted the original—that is, civic-minded—civil rights argument, he had never changed it, even though the entire political spectrum shifted around him. Group-mindedness may employ the language of rights, but it is the enemy of the understanding of rights that shaped American law and American habits.

Affirmative action, which is a fancy name for compensatory discrimination, also sins against use. It awards credentials to those who don't deserve them and devalues the achievements of those who would have earned the credentials anyway. Every black musician in the Detroit symphony orchestra must face the question, Is he there because he is a musician, or a "musician"? A musician, or a black? Affirmative action establishes bureaucratic judgments over ability, and political skill in prying them out of reluctant bureaucracies over work. It favors "leaders" over the led; those who talk over those who try to do a job; the Jesse Jacksons of the world over honest people.

The two great arguments in favor of group-mindedness are that it is temporary and self-liquidating, and that it leads to social peace. Groups, it is said, need special attention to their needs in order to boost their members onto the ladder of success; until the members of the favored group reach the rungs, they need special recognition so that they will not feel discontented—to the point of violence in the sixties, to the point of apathy today. Both arguments are specious, because group-mindedness has no way of limiting itself. It can never say that it has worked. Any group demand might be legitimate, so there is no end to the process. Definitions of failure will be altered and expanded; thus, feminists want not only equal access to jobs, but equal pay for different jobs which they deem to be equivalent. Peace never comes. Yugoslavia has practiced group-mindedness for forty years, and the fruit is Kosovo.

Assailing group politics will earn Bush storms of disapproval every time he does it, and no immediate or obvious approval—necessarily so, because the group is, by definition, mobilized. But it is essential if he is serious about a return to civic-mindedness.

A great challenge to civic-mindedness is immigration, legal and illegal, which has been booming for more than a decade—not as high in percentage terms as the peak years of the turn of the century, but within the same order of magnitude. Mexican national holidays are now as big a deal in Texas as they are in Nueva Leon. That's all right, so long as they become as harmless as Steuben Day. The best favor America can do its newcomers is to present them with a clear sense of what America is, and what they should become. WASPification is their road to success. To treat new immigrants as patches in the national quilt is to relegate them to being patches in the sewing box.

English-only laws are an obvious answer, though they must be applied with care. The market, which on the whole is a great anglicizing force, will also preserve other tongues wherever they don't get in the way of social advancement: Chinatowns that have existed for more than a hundred years still have signs in Chinese. State option should also be preserved. As a former governor of New Hampshire, Sununu knows that the signs that greet motorists at the border say *Bienvenue à* (lower case), as well as WELCOME TO, New Hampshire. But English still is, and should be, the majority language, the lingua franca, the language of law. Schools should teach it as early and as thoroughly as possible. Partisans of bilingual education claim that it is in fact the best way to give a kid a good grounding in basic skills, including English. The burden of proof must be on them.

Immigration is good, because a dynamic economy can always use new people. But the people we want aren't permanent immigrants, but future WASPs, so to speak.

There is a group of Americans that needs WASPifying even more desperately than immigrants. That is the urban poor. The poverty programs of the Great Society were a massive program of de-assimilation, of fighting poverty without changing poor people. The underclass is the result, though the very word "underclass" is part of the problem, for the worst thing we can do to the people we use the term to denote is to treat them as a class, economically or characterologically locked into their plight. Treating them so will keep them there. For those who believe that industry and antisensuality can lift them out of it, the class barriers will give way. The Nation of Islam preaches this message, which is why it is so successful and, to this extent, admirable. It also preaches that nonblack races are the demonic results of a prehistoric breeding experiment on the island of Patmos, which is why it should not be encouraged. It ought to be possible to impart uplifting habits without race hatred.

The poor, and the not-so-poor, have a drug problem. Since the WASPs' last bright idea for handling a drug problem was Prohibition, their guidance may be considered suspect. (What the Bush administration is now pursuing is prohibition without the Protestant touch, and it's working about as well as it worked for alcohol.) They should have trusted more to the force of habit and example. The early history of gin offers an interesting comparison, for gin was the heroin of eighteenth-century London, cutting through the English lower classes, whose experience of alcohol had been limited to beer and mead, like a scythe. Parliament tried prohibition, to no effect. Drunkenness diminished when England became more prosperous, and more evangelical—Methodism had its greatest success in the lower classes—in a word, more Victorian. There continued to be wretched, self-destroying drunkards, as there will always be wretched drug addicts. But instilling a sense of something to work for, and a consequent horror of self-indulgence, is the best way to diminish their numbers.

Some of these questions, Bush might be interested to know, came up at a policy luncheon sponsored by a New York think tank during the last mayoral election. Over coffee, the policy types became embroiled in a rather abstract discussion of educational systems, when one of the journalists present broke in impatiently: "What about the underclass?" What about the fifteen-year-old girls with babies, he elaborated, children with children? How do you propose to help *them*? It was one of those don't-just-do-something, stand-there questions that are supposed to make everyone gape with a sense of his own frivolity and inadequacy. Most of the discussants gaped. One, however, a former chancellor of the Board of Education, answered elegantly and compellingly: The best thing a school can do, for the fifteen-year-old mother and the fifteen-year-old not-yet-a-mother alike, is—teach them. If they have something to work at and for, they won't get into trouble in the first place, or they won't get into more of it. The best sex education, and drug education, is the three R's and an ethos in which the three R's are seen as central—that is, useful.

All of these are, in part, political problems. There is also the overarching political problem, which is our inability to make any rational fit between means and ends. We are unable because our ends have become endless. Bush's predecessor, the most popular president since FDR, was elected as an avowed foe of overgrown government, yet government only grew during his eight years in office, on both the military and the domestic side. This is because Ronald Reagan was unable, or unwilling, to renounce progressive politics, the politics of going with the flow. American politics was once definitional. It believed that man was something specific and unchangeable, and that from his nature the proper tasks of the state might be deduced. At least, American politicians once talked as if they believed that, and their talk affected their practice. Returning to that lost mental universe would not be the end of conflict: All the births and deaths of major American parties occurred before the Progressive onslaught. So did the Civil War. But at least politics was about something, instead of everything.

One crucial question is beyond Bush's purview, except as an interested individual: What should the Protestant churches do? Since we ascribed baleful, even tragic consequences to the century-long schism between modernizers and traditionalists, the obvious goal would seem to be unity. Obvious, but mistaken. There has been a surfeit of unity talk for the last thirty years. The Commission on Church Union, begun by the late Bishop James Pike and still carrying on, is the great engine of it. It is, among other things, one of the great real estate scams of the century, since if the major mainline denominations ever did fuse, they would reap a fortune from the windfall sale of redundant urban churches. In fact, such pipe dreams only encourage the stasis of the mainline. While historic denominations like the Reformed Church talk, they are surpassed in size by upstarts like the Church of God of Cleveland, Tennessee. What American Protestantism needs, for its own good and everybody's, is a period of religious warfare. It throve, within a cultural consensus, during the years when ministers with pulpits traded insults with open-air circuit riders, and denominations wrangled over baptism and free will. Let the two sides of the schism thwack each other. Above all, let the elements within each group assert their claims against each other. The Anglican Orthodox Church and the Primitive Baptists may both be traditionalists, but they represent rather different traditions. Let's hear about them. The Moody Bible Institute, a fundamentalist seminary in Chicago, recently blasted assorted televangelists, including Pat Robertson, for misunderstanding original sin, while a national evangelical campus group has affiliated itself with Eastern Orthodoxy. Promising signs. Out of conflict, a restored cultural amalgam will emerge. The Protestant churches became too enamored of the idea of their moral authority. While they were focused on the idea, they lost the authority. When they focus again on the truth, the authority will return.

Is George Bush the man to lead a WASP renaissance? Barbara Bush caused a jag in the sales of faux pearls. Will her husband start a run on true ideas?

For a few months during the off-year election of 1982, I helped write speeches for Vice President Bush part-time. My main task was to tinker with the stump speech. Were we going into industrial Ohio (the election was held in the depth of a recession)? Emphasize the good economic news—what there was of it. Campaigning for a liberal Republican? Steer clear of the social issues. The one speech I worked on from the ground up was an address Bush was to give to a conference of the Episcopal Church, his church, in New Orleans. For a large part of the audience, it was a hard sell. The Reagan administration was not exactly the ideal presidency of St. John the Divine. Sitting in the back of the auditorium, one could watch delegates scoffing at their fellow Episcopalian. Bush, knowing it or perhaps sensing it from the lectern, was determined to make his case. In the best of circumstances, inept pauses clog Bush's sentences, like double-parked cars. This was worse, for in the heat of the moment he improvised—long loops that turned out to be verbless, like a gymnast grabbing in mid-spin for a ring that isn't there. He came through the experience on sheer earnestness, which won some of the crowd over. Much of it had been in his corner from the start—in part, I supposed, for institutional reasons. For Bush is a devout churchgoer, having belonged, like the members of many moderate and liberal Protestant denominations, to a parish—St. Anne's in Kennebunkport—which proceeds untroubled by the antics at the top.

Bush is also married to his first wife, and all but one of their children are married to first spouses. They see each other often. Bush's family prompted Digby Baltzell, first scholarly arraigner of WASPs, wistfully to ask if it wouldn't be a good thing if more American boys married the first girls they kissed.[1]

The contrast was often noted between all of this and the private life of Ronald Reagan, who talked about old-fashioned values but rarely saw several of his children, even more rarely went to church, and was divorced from his first wife forty-two years ago.

But public life is more than the private lives of public figures. In this dimension, Bush falls short of what is needful. He has little eloquence or public force of personality. (The irony about Reagan talking such a good moral game cuts two ways.) His powers of articulation are rarely more than competent. Though he is a curious and open-minded man, he shows no intellectual depth. This hardly makes him unique among American politicians. Actually to sit down and listen to one of the few who are reputed to be smart—Bill Bradley, for instance—is torture. Intellectuals and intellectualoids make the inner circle now and then—Theodore Sorensen, Jeane Kirkpatrick. They are also not very competent politicians.

Throughout his career, George Bush has been a lucky—almost eerily lucky—man. His enemies have self-destructed or have become friends, and his friends have been legion. His first year in the White House passed in a blur of events—Havel, Kohl, and Chamorro doing their turns; tyrants shooting Chinese students, and Rumanians shooting tyrants—that, though it gave him little to do, virtually ensured that he could not do anything wrong.

But luck is nothing to count on. America's luck, in any case, has not been as good as his. The country has problems which, if they grow worse, or if he fails to address them, will become identified, and properly so, with him.

Bush won the opportunity to deal with them not because of Ralph Lauren, but because the public had a hope, based in part on what it gathered from his private life, that he could bring WASP virtues to bear on them. The WASP character has been dirtied for sixty years, and a lot of the dirt has stuck. But since it is the only character we have ever had, we are still attracted even to inklings of it.

No one has a right to rule America. But if WASPs reclaim their values—or if anyone else claims them—they will have an obligation to offer themselves as leaders, and they will be accepted.

Because of the peculiar circumstances of its origin and development, America has created and often enough realized the pattern of a society dynamic but steady, open but consistent, free but moral, prosperous but just. Better patterns may appear one day, but they are unimaginable now. We mentioned the combination of pride and humility that can prompt WASP retreat. The WASPs' return will also require pride and humility: pride in what America has accomplished in this world, under their guidance, and the humility of continuing to maintain it, not for the sake of their own self-esteem but because it is right.

Notes

Chapter 1
Bush-Bashing, WASP-Bashing

1. Walt Harrington, "Born to Run," *The Washington Post Magazine*, September 28, 1986.
2. Margaret Garrard Warner, "Bush Battles the 'Wimp Factor,'" *Newsweek*, October 19, 1987.
3. George Bush, with Victor Gold, *Looking Forward* (New York: Doubleday, 1987), pp. 26–27.
4. Warner.
5. Barry Bearak, "Team Player Bush: A Yearning to Serve," *Los Angeles Times*, November 22, 1987.
6. Bush, p. 43.
7. *Ibid.*, p. 205.
8. Richard Cohen, *Washington Post*, October 16, 1988.
9. Jonathan Alter, *Newsweek*, July 4, 1988.
10. One Bushwoman crossed the line: Loretta Lynn told a heartland audience that she thought Dukakis was hard to pronounce.
11. Alessandra Stanley, "Presidency by Ralph Lauren," *The New Republic*, December 12, 1988.
12. *The Vintage Mencken* (New York: Vintage Books, 1955), pp. 132, 130; H. L. Mencken, *Prejudices: A Selection* (New York: Vintage Books, 1958), p. 99.
13. D. H. Lawrence, *Studies in Classic American Literature* (New York: Viking Press, 1964), pp. 14, 19.
14. John P. Marquand, *Point of No Return* (Chicago: Academy Chicago Publishers, 1985), p. 55.
15. Dwight Macdonald, *Against the American Grain* (New York: Random House, 1962), pp. 197–99.
16. Robert Lowell, "During Fever" and "Waking in the Blue," *Life Studies* (New York: Farrar, Straus & Giroux, 1959).

17. Norman Mailer, *Advertisements for Myself* (New York: G. P. Putnam's, Berkeley Medallion, 1959), pp. 357, 329, 321–22.
18. E. Digby Baltzell, *The Protestant Establishment* (New Haven: Yale University Press, 1987), pp. ix–x.
19. Eldridge Cleaver, *Soul on Ice* (New York: Mc-Graw Hill, 1968), p. 81.
20. Norman Podhoretz, *Making It* (New York: Random House, 1967), p. 149.
21. Garry Wills, *Nixon Agonistes* (New York: Mentor, 1971), p. 176.
22. Michael Novak, *The Rise of the Unmeltable Ethnics* (New York: Macmillan, 1971), pp. xxii, 107.
23. Ben Stein, *The View from Sunset Boulevard* (New York: Basic Books, 1979), pp. 70–71, 67.
24. "Ringing the Bells," from Anne Sexton, *The Complete Poems* (Boston: Houghton Mifflin, 1981). Martha Bayles reminded me what the Doors's lyrics were like. No one had to remind me what the music was like.
25. Peter Schrag, *The Decline of the WASP* (New York: Simon & Schuster, 1970), pp. 188, 18.
26. Norman Mailer, *Miami and the Siege of Chicago* (New York: New American Library, 1968), p. 35.
27. Richard C. Robertiello, MD, and Diana Hoguet, *The Wasp Mystique* (New York: Donald I. Fine, 1987), p. 106.
28. Robert C. Christopher, *Crashing the Gates* (New York: Simon & Schuster, 1989), p. 29.
29. *The Vintage Mencken* (note 12 above), pp. 158–59
30. John Updike, *Roger's Version* (New York: Fawcett Crest, 1986), p. 80.
31. Hendrik Hertzberg, "The End Is Nigh," *The New Republic*, November 12, 1984, and "Robertson's Oedipus Complex," *The New Republic*, March 28, 1988.
32. John Murray Cuddihy, *No Offense* (New York: Seabury Press, 1978), p. 52.
33. Paul Fussell, *Class* (New York: Ballantine Books, 1984).
34. J. Hector St. John de Crèvecoeur, quoted in Sidney E. Mead, *The Lively Experiment* (New York: Harper & Row, 1976), p. 14.

Chapter 2
Who Are These People?

1. Louis Auchincloss, *The Embezzler* (New York: Dell Publishing Co., Inc., 1967), p. 32.
2. Interview with Digby Baltzell.
3. Interview with Bruce Chapman.
4. Stanley Lieberson and Mary C. Water, *From Many Strands* (New York: Russell Sage Foundation, 1988), p. 37.
5. Interview with Joseph Adelson.

6. See Edwin S. Harwood, "Work and Community Among Urban New-comers," unpublished, University of Chicago, 1966.

7. Interview with John Lukacs.

8. J. C. Furnas, *The Americans* (New York: G. P. Putnam's Sons, 1969), p. 127.

9. See Thomas L. Purvis, "The European Ancestry of the United States Population, 1790," *William and Mary Quarterly*, January 1984, and Forrest McDonald and Ellen Shapiro McDonald, "The Ethnic Origins of the American People, 1790," *William and Mary Quarterly*, April 1980.

10. Thomas Jefferson, letter to Henry Lee, May 18, 1825, *The Life and Selected Writings of Thomas Jefferson* (New York, Modern Library, 1944), p. 719.

11. For Trenchard and Gordon, see Bernard Bailyn, *The Origins of American Politics* (New York: Random House, 1970). For Scottish philosophers, see Garry Wills, *Inventing America* (New York: Random House, 1979). For Locke as a modern see Leo Strauss, *Natural Right and History* (Chicago: University of Chicago Press, 1965).

12. George Santayana, *Character and Opinion in the United States* (New York: Charles Scribner's Sons, 1920), p. 194

13. The first census counted 3.9 million Americans in 1790. The population in 1780 has been put at 2.8 million. Margo J. Anderson, *The American Census* (New Haven: Yale University Press, 1988), pp. 11, 14. The Catholic total was the figure of Bishop John Carroll of Baltimore, quoted by Edwin Scott Gaustad, *Historical Atlas of Religion in America* (New York: Harper & Row, 1962), p. 36. For Jews, see Sydney E. Ahlstrom, *A Religious History of the American People* (New Haven: Yale University Press, 1972), p. 573.

14. John Updike, *Picked-up Pieces* (New York: Fawcett Crest, 1977). p. 28.

15. Ahlstrom guessed that the percentage of "people whose forebears bore the 'stamp of Geneva' in some broader sense" was as high as 85 or 90—though, since this figure puts the "stamp of Geneva" on all Anglicans, it is too high. Ahlstrom, p. 124.

16. *Ibid.*, p. 177.

17. *Ibid.*, p. 128.

18. For the frontier argument, see Mead (Chapter 1 above, note 34).

19. Paul Johnson, in *Unsecular America*, ed. Richard John Neuhaus (Grand Rapids, Mich.: Eerdmans, 1987), p. 5.

20. Alexis de Tocqueville, *Democracy in America* (New York: Vintage Books, 1945), vol. I, p. 315. The figures on church membership are from Theodore Caplow, Howard M. Bahr, and Bruce Chadwick, *All Faithful People* (Minneapolis: University of Minnesota Press, 1983), p. 29.

21. Benjamin Franklin, *The Autobiography and Other Writings* (New York: Bantam Books, 1982), p. 266.
22. David Hackett Fischer, *Albion's Seed* (New York: Oxford University Press, 1989), pp. 220–22. Fischer argues that there were not just two British character types in colonial America, but four—East Anglian Puritans in New England, southern English Cavaliers on the shores of Chesapeake Bay, North Midland Quakers in the Delaware Valley, and a border type, drawn from the old Scottish–English frontier and Ulster, and scattered through the Appalachian back country. He also argues that these four types run through American culture and history, maintaining their distinctness to this day, so that Barry Goldwater, though he is of Jewish ancestry, upholds the politics of the back country, while Walter Fauntroy is by style, temperament, and surname a Virginia gentleman, albeit a black one. *Albion's Seed* is a fascinating book. As a general theory of the American character, however, it seems to me to beg the question, Why was there one country, nor four?
23. McDonald and McDonald (note 9 above).
24. Mencken, *Prejudices: A Selection* (Chapter 1 above, note 13), p. 76–77.

Chapter 3
The Way of the Wasp

1. Franklin (Chapter 2 above, note 21), pp. 84, 77.
2. Ralph Waldo Emerson, *The Portable Emerson* (New York: Viking Penguin, 1981), p. 11.
3. Cuddihy (Chapter 1 above, note 32), p. 17.
4. George Nash, *The Life of Herbert Hoover* (New York: W. W. Norton, 1983), vol. I, p. 3.
5. *The Federalist Papers* (New York: New American Library, 1961), p. 322.
6. Podhoretz (Chapter 1 above, note 20), p. 55.
7. Joseph Addison, *Cato*, Act I, scene ii.
8. Owen Johnson, *Stover at Yale* (New York: Collier Books, 1968), p. 19.
9. Tocqueville (Chapter 2 above, note 20), p. 314.
10. William James, *Pragmatism*, quoted in Will Durant, *The Story of Philosophy* (New York: Time Inc., 1962), p. 476.
11. H. G. Wells, *Mr. Britling Sees It Through* (New York: Macmillan, 1916), p. 33.
12. Franklin, pp. 81–82.
13. Quoted in John Lukacs, *Outgrowing Democracy* (Garden City, N.Y.: Doubleday, 1984), p. 37.
14. Quoted in Stephen Garney, *Gramercy Park* (New York: Rutledge Books, 1984), p. 131.

15. Alex Comfort, author of the book, not the parody, was an English-man, but his book found its way into many bedrooms here.
16. Santayana (Chapter 2 above, note 12), p. 6.
17. Anthony Trollope, *Phineas Redux* (New York: Oxford University Press, 1983), p. 269.

Chapter 4
Others, and the WASP World They Aspire To

1. Quoted in Anderson (Chapter 2 above, note 13), p. 146.
2. Nathan Glazer and Daniel P. Moynihan, *Beyond the Melting Pot* (Cambridge, Mass.: MIT Press, 1970), p. 56.
3. *Ibid.*, p. 312.
4. Luigi Barzini, *O America* (New York: Penguin, 1977), p. 174–75.
5. John Updike, *Trust Me,* (New York: Knopf, 1987), p. 198.
6. Samuel Beckett, *Molloy* (New York: Grove Press, 1955), p. 161.
7. Interview with John Roche.
8. Ernest Hemingway, *The Essential Hemingway* (Harmondsworth, Middlesex: Penguin Books, 1964), p. 318.
9. Glazer and Moynihan, p. 275.
10. Mencken, *Prejudices: A Selection* (Chapter 1 above, note 13), pp. 124–25.
11. Baltzell (Chapter 1 above, note 18), p. 138.
12. Ahlstrom (Chapter 2 above, note 13), p. 917, and Lukacs (Chapter 3 above, note 13), p. 128.
13. Will Herberg, *Protestant-Catholic-Jew* (Garden City, N.Y.: Doubleday, 1960), p. 252.
14. John P. Marquand, *The Late George Apley* (New York: Washington Square Press, 1963), p. 235.
15. Lukacs, pp. 134, 150. The vermin line is Owen Wister's; the inner light, Bliss Perry's.
16. Schrag (Chapter 1 above, note 25), p. 20.

Chapter 5
WASPs, and Other Worlds They Aspire To

1. Henry Adams, *The Education of Henry Adams* (Boston: Houghton Mifflin, 1969), pp. 15–16, 46.
2. Nash (Chapter 3 above, note 8), p. 498.
3. Adams, p. 232.
4. *Ibid.*, pp. xxiii 211, 303.
5. *Ibid.*, p. 321, and Leon Edel, *The Life of Henry James,* vol. III (New York: Avon Books, 1978), p. 30.
6. Adams, p. 338.
7. *Ibid.*, pp. 62–63.

8. *Basic Selections from Emerson* (New York: New American Library, 1954), p. 11.
9. *The Portable Emerson* (Chapter 3 above, note 2), p. 7.
10. *Ibid.,* p. 153.
11. *Ibid.,* pp. 149, 229.
12. *Ibid.,* p. 190.
13. *Ibid.,* pp. 158, 78.
14. Baltzell (Chapter 1 above, note 18), p. 181.
15. Woodrow Wilson, *Selected Literary and Political Papers and Addresses,* vol. I (New York: Grosset & Dunlap: 1926), p. 1; *The Papers of Woodrow Wilson,* vol. 4 (Princeton, N.J.: Princeton University Press, 1968), pp. 154, 171.
16. Arthur S. Link, *Woodrow Wilson: A Brief Biography* (Cleveland: World Publishing, 1963), pp. 30, 36.
17. *The Papers,* vol. 21, p. 409.
18. Woodrow Wilson, *Constitutional Government in the United States* (New York: Columbia University Press, 1961), p. 5.
19. Woodrow Wilson, *Leaders of Men* (Princeton, N.J.: Princeton University Press, 1952), pp. 47–48.
20. Wilson, *Constitutional Government,* pp. 4, 69.
21. Charles Kesler, "Woodrow Wilson and the Statesmanship of Progress," in Thomas B. Silver and Peter W. Schramm, eds. *Natural Right and Political Right* (Durham, N.C.: Carolina Academic Press, 1984), p. 105. Kesler first showed me what Wilson was up to, and his essay deserves study, as will his book on Wilson when he finally writes it.
22. Wilson, *Constitutional Government,* p. 79.
23. "The South," wrote Allen Tate, "did not realize its genius in time, but continued to defend itself on the political terms of the North," while "its religious impulse was inarticulate . . . because it tried to encompass its destiny within the terms of Protestantism. . . . The Southern politicians could merely quote Scripture to defend slavery, the while they defended their society as a whole with the catchwords of eighteenth-century politics. And this is why the South separated from the North too late, and so lost its cause." *I'll Take My Stand* (Baton Rouge: Louisiana State University Press, 1977), p. 168.
24. Jack Kerouac, *On the Road* (New York: New American Library, 1985), p. 148. The sentence goes on: " . . . feeling that the best the white world had offered was not enough ecstasy for me, not enough life, joy, kicks, darkness, music, not enough night."
25. Jack Curry, *Woodstock: The Summer of Our Lives* (New York: Weidenfeld & Nicolson, 1989), p. xx.
26. See Stanley Rothman and S. Robert Lichter, *Roots of Radicalism* (New York: Oxford University Press, 1982).
27. *Washington Post,* February 13, 1984.

Chapter 6
Wall Street, at Home and Abroad

1. Richard Norton Smith, *Thomas E. Dewey and His Times* (New York: Simon & Schuster, 1982), p. 387.
2. E. Digby Baltzell, *Philadelphia Gentlemen* (New York: Free Press, 1958), p. 266.
3. Connie Bruck, *The Predator's Ball* (New York: The American Lawyer, Simon & Schuster, 1988), p. 331.
4. *New York Times,* January 31, 1987.
5. Interviews with Ken Lipper and Evan Galbraith.
6. Ken Auletta, *Greed and Glory on Wall Street* (New York: Warner Books, 1987), pp. 10, 14.
7. Interview with Ken Lipper.
8. George F. Kennan, *American Diplomacy 1900–1950* (New York: Mentor Books, 1952), p. 80.
9. Philip C. Jessup, *Elihu Root* (New York: Dodd, Mead, 1938), vol. I, p. 215.
10. *Ibid.,* vol. I, p. 434.
11. Henry Stimson and McGeorge Bundy, *On Active Service in Peace and War* (New York: Harper, 1947), p. xviii.
12. *Ibid.,* p. xxii.
13. Baltzell, *The Protestant Establishment* (Chapter 1 above, note 18), p. 113.
14. Baltzell, *Philadelphia Gentlemen,* p. 390.
15. *New York Times,* September 30, 1952.
16. Merlo J. Pusey, *Charles Evans Hughes* (New York: Columbia University Press, 1963), vol. I, p. 113.
17. Jessup, vol. I, p. 59.
18. Mead (Chapter 1 above, note 34), p. 160.
19. Henry Kissinger, *Years of Upheaval* (Boston: Little, Brown, 1982), p. 432.
20. Kennan (note 8 above), pp. 83–84.
21. Smith (note 1 above), p. 382, and Steve Neal, *Dark Horse* (Garden City, N.Y.: Doubleday, 1984), p. 264.
22. *The Institutional Investor,* June 1987.
23. Interview with Francois de Saint Phalle.
24. Interview with Francois de Saint Phalle.
25. Interview with Evan Galbraith.

Chapter 7
Artists in Exile

1. John Updike, *Rabbit Run* (Greenwich, Conn.: Fawcett Crest, 1960), pp. 9–11.
2. *Ibid.,* p. 26.

3. John Updike, *Hugging the Shore* (New York: Vintage Books, 1984), p. 877.
4. Updike, *Picked-up Pieces* (Chapter 2 above, note 14), p. 491.
5. John Updike, *Self-Consciousness* (New York: Knopf, 1989), pp. 129, 183.
6. Ahlstrom (Chapter 2 above, note 13), p. 939.
7. Updike, *Rabbit Run*, p. 159.
8. Updike, *Picked-up Pieces*, p. 13; John Updike, *Assorted Prose* (New York: Fawcett Crest, 1966), pp. 214, 212, 218.
9. John Updike, *A Month of Sundays* (New York: Fawcett Crest, 1976), p. 109.
10. Vivian Perlis, *Charles Ives Remembered* (New York: W. W. Norton, 1976), p. 82.
11. *Ibid.*, p. 16.
12. Charles Ives, *Essays Before a Sonata, The Majority, and Other Writings* (New York: W. W. Norton, 1962), p. 111.
13. Henry David Thoreau, *Walden* (New York: Harper & Row, 1965), p. 92.
14. Perlis, p. 219.
15. Ives, p. 210.
16. *Ibid.*, p. 237.
17. Perlis, p. 158.
18. *Ibid.*, pp. 87, 16.
19. Henry and Sidney Cowell make this argument in *Charles Ives and His Music* (New York: Oxford University Press, 1955).
20. Perlis, p. 82.

Chapter 8
Losing the Faith

1. Baltzell, *Philadelphia Gentlemen* (Chapter 6 above, note 2) p. 236.
2. *Ibid.*, p. 232.
3. *Ibid.*, p. 235.
4. Perlis (Chapter 7 above, note 10), p. 88; John Updike, *A Month of Sundays* (Chapter 7 above, note 9), p. 246.
5. Richard John Neuhaus, *The Naked Public Square* (Grand Rapids, Mich.: W. B. Eerdmans, 1984), p. 207.
6. Wade Clark Roof and William McKinney, *American Mainline Religion* (New Brunswick, N.J.: Rutgers University Press, 1988), p. 88.
7. *Ibid.*, p. 87.
8. Ahlstrom (Chapter 2 above, note 13), p. 381.
9. Charles M. Sheldon, *In His Steps* (Springdale, Pa.: Whitaker House, 1979), pp. 146, 124.
10. Ahlstrom, p. 786, and Sheldon, p. 250.
11. It should be noted that an upper-class slice of Protestants—what

Joseph Alsop called "the WASP Ascendancy"—opposed Prohibition. Pierre du Pont (not the presidential candidate, but an earlier one) backed FDR in 1932 (though he would later support the bitterly anti–New Deal Liberty League) because Roosevelt was a wet. George Apley kept a bootlegger. But Protestant clergymen, high and low, were virtually unanimous in being dry. German Lutherans were the only significant exception.

12. Ahlstrom, pp. 871, 925.
13. *Ibid.,* p. 922.
14. Richard Weaver, *The Ethics of Rhetoric* (Chicago: Henry Regnery Company, 1953), chapter II.
15. *The Vintage Mencken* (Chapter 1 above, note 12), p. 161.
16. Herberg (Chapter 4 above, note 13), p. 123.
17. *Life,* July 1, 1957. Graham was defended by a mainline clergyman, John Sutherland Bonnell, the pastor of the Fifth Avenue Presbyterian Church in New York, though even he registered a reservation: Graham showed "no sufficient recognition of un-Christian social conditions and practices in our city and nation."
18. Interview with James Davison Hunter.
19. See Updike, *Hugging the Shore* (Chapter 7 above, note 3), p. 829.
20. Dinesh D'Souza, *Falwell Before the Millennium* (Chicago: Regnery Gateway, 1984), pp. 99, 111.
21. Roof and McKinney (note 6 above), p. 188.
22. Robert Lerner, Stanley Rothman, and S. Robert Lichter, "Christian Religious Elites," in *Public Opinion,* March–April 1989.
23. Richard Brookhiser, "Pat Robertson Seeks Lower Office," *National Review,* August 29, 1986.
24. Roof and McKinney, p. 178.
25. Cuddihy (Chapter 1 above, note 32), p. 6.
26. Christopher (Chapter 1 above, note 28), p. 178.
27. Caplow *et al.* (Chapter 2 above, note 20), p. 126.
28. *Ibid.,* p. 299, and Neuhaus, *Unsecular America* (Chapter 2 above, note 19), pp. 15–16.

Chapter 9
Three Places in the Middle Atlantic States

1. Information for this chapter came from Kenneth E. Hasbrouck and Erma R. DeWitt, *The Street of the Huguenots* (privately printed, 1952); Kenneth E. Hasbrouck, *The Huguenot with Emphasis upon the Huguenots of New Paltz* (New Paltz, N.Y.: Huguenot Historical Society, 1970); *Our French Church* (Crispell Family Association, 1973); Larry E. Burgess, *Mohonk: Its People and Spirit* (Smiley Brothers, 1980); Richard E. Brewer, *Perspectives on Ocean Grove* (Historical Society of Ocean Grove,

N.J., 1969); the prologue of Jeffrey Hart, *From This Moment On* (New York: Crown Publishers, 1987); and "In Tents by the Sea, an Annual Revival of the Spirit," *The New York Times,* July 6, 1989.

Chapter 10
The Post-WASP World, and How We Got Here

1. Franklin (Chapter 2 above, note 21) p. 118.
2. Standard stump oratory. See John Kenneth White, *The New Politics of Old Values* (Hanover, N.H.: University Press of New England, 1988).
3. Henry James, *The Bostonians,* in *Novels 1881–1886* (New York: Library of America, 1985), p. 825.
4. Theodore H. White, *The Making of the President: 1968* (New York: Pocket Books, 1970), pp. 496–97.
5. John Updike, *Couples* (New York: Fawcett Crest, 1968), p. 114.
6. Mark Krupnick, *Lionel Trilling and the Fate of Cultural Criticism* (Evanston, Ill.: Northwestern University Press, 1986), pp. 48, 50.
7. *Ibid.,* p. 37.
8. Diana Trilling, "Lionel Trilling, A Jew at Columbia," *Commentary,* March 1979, p. 44.
9. Krupnick, pp. 40–41.
10. Trilling, pp. 45–46.
11. Krupnick, p. 146.
12. *Ibid.,* p. 37.

Chapter 11
Can the Way of the WASP Be Saved?

1. Herberg (Chapter 4 above, note 13), p. 128.

Chapter 12
Can the Way of the WASP Save America?

1. E. Digby Baltzell, "Blue-Blood Blues," *The New Republic,* April 3, 1989.

Index